HEWARD GRAFFTEY

WHY CANADIANS GET THE POLITICIANS & GOVERNMENTS THEY DON'T WANT

Stoddart

*This book is dedicated
with much love and deep affection
to my three children:
Arthur Heward, Clement Tae Yong,
and Leah Yoon Hee*

Copyright © 1991 by Heward Grafftey

All rights reserved. No part of this publication may be reproduced or transmitted in any form or by any means, electronic or mechanical, including photocopying, recording, or any information storage and retrieval system, without permission in writing from the publisher.

First published in 1991 by
Stoddart Publishing Co. Limited
34 Lesmill Road
Toronto, Canada
M3B 2T6

Canadian Cataloguing in Publication Data
Grafftey, Heward, 1928-
　Why Canadians get the politicians and governments they don't want

Includes index.
ISBN 0-7737-2519-9

1. Politics, Practical — Canada. 2. Nominations for office — Canada. 3. Political participation — Canada. 4. Canada — Politics and government — 1984- .*

JL196.G73 1991　324'.0971　C91-094806-2

COVER DESIGN: Brant Cowie / ArtPlus Limited

Printed and bound in the United States of America

Contents

Preface *v*

1 The Need for Reform *1*

Part One: How We Nominate Party Candidates *11*

2 Getting Grass-Roots Experience *13*
3 Transition to Power *24*

Part Two: How We Nominate Party Leaders *35*

4 Looking Back *37*
5 Looking South and Abroad *54*
6 Stanfield and Clark *73*
7 The Fall of Clark and the Rise of Mulroney *89*
8 Recommendations for Reform *110*

Part Three: Who Controls the Purse Strings? *121*

9 Taxation without Representation *123*
10 Disastrous Budgets and Defeated Governments *136*

Part Four: Bureaucratic Control *149*

11 Majority Government 1958 *151*
12 Minority Government 1979 *163*

Part Five: Some Unfinished Business *185*

13 A Modern Constitution for Modern Times *187*
14 More Unfinished Business *199*

Index *208*

PREFACE

On the weekend of June 23, 1990, the Meech Lake initiative unofficially died, and Jean Chrétien was elected leader of the Liberal party. Meech Lake represented a historic constitutional watershed. Chrétien's election was a landmark involving the leadership of a great national party. Yet, something seemed amiss. A troubled citizenry read their papers, listened to their radios, and watched their TVs with a deep sense of misgiving and cynicism. Instead of participating in these events, they were relegated to the sidelines. Meech Lake was strictly a matter of wheeling and dealing behind closed doors. Chrétien's nomination — like Mulroney's and McLaughlin's — was the result of an élitist and outmoded leadership-selection process that purposely excluded public participation. Both events flew in the face of basic principles of freedom and democracy, where broad public participation is a "must." Yet I remain optimistic and sense a serious grass-roots reaction, one that demands openness, public consultation, and participation in fundamental constitutional change and the selection of national party leaders. Trusting the people does not constitute unbridled populism. It does, however, constitute redressing the balance in a country that pretends to be free.

How do we nominate party candidates for office? Is there enough involvement by individuals to ensure that candidates are chosen democratically by a broadly based membership of the party in each constituency?

Do our elected representatives control the purse strings — or does complete control now rest in the hands of an unresponsive bureaucracy? Do our elections effect much change if politicians are always running for office, while leaving policy and the management of the country to permanent officials?

Often I am reminded of what can be referred to as "the law of sycophancy." Leaders never know when the jig is up. Who's telling Mulroney that he must go now, before it's too late, before he ruins not only his party, but his country? People tell me that I'm unrealistic, that we can't have a leadership convention before the next election. But, what could be more unrealistic than going into an election at a time when the union is threatened, when we must renew our federalism with a new constitution, but with leaders that nobody wants?

I well remember a colleague who often visited me in my offices in Parliament Hill's West Block. He would damn Diefenbaker up and down. "Dief is an unholy menace," he would reiterate. "He must go." One day, Dief dropped by my office for a chat. My colleague was already with me. On seeing Dief, he leaped up. "Mr. Leader," he exclaimed. "You're doing a great job. Carry on." Such is life on the banks of the Rideau. Power corrupts; absolute power corrupts absolutely.

One thing that truly differentiates the political parties of Canada is the type of people they attract. When I joined my party in the mid-1950s, I thought I was joining a "progressive conservative" party, progressive in social policy and conservative in economic policy. The Liberal government had been in power for twenty-two years. People said it could stay in power forever, that one-party rule by the Liberal party, long since grown arrogant in its primacy, was not incompatible with democratic principle. While still adhering to progressive principles, I feel as if I have been duped and conned. My party has always been dominated by right-wing Neanderthals who crucified Diefenbaker, patronized Stanfield, and ridiculed Clark. When I joined the Progressive Conservatives, I felt my party could be creative in terms of progressive social policy. There were those who felt that only Liberals and socialists could be

PREFACE

activist, that Conservatives were called upon to govern only when the people wanted to maintain the status quo and to retrench. I didn't believe it then and still don't, but since 1984, Brian Mulroney has given me nothing with which to reinforce my argument. Whatever his instincts and convictions, Mulroney gained the leadership aided and abetted by the entire right wing of his party. Like Reagan's in the United States, his tenure has catered to an era of greed where the gap between upper- and lower-income Canadians has widened. Mulroney made a deal with the few and cannot legislate for the "many," just as he made a deal with Quebec separatists and has never been able to define and defend the federal cause.

Today, we make no pretence at nominating party leaders and candidates for the Commons in a free, open, and truly democratic way. Bureaucratic control of government and constitution-making behind closed doors fly in the face of democratic principles. I have drawn from my experience in public life to outline and describe the present state of affairs relating to all these considerations. The need for immediate reform is obvious. If the reader finds my proposals for reform both positive and constructive — if these proposals prove to be of service to Canada and its people — this book will not have been written in vain.

My first words of thanks go to Michael O'Neill who, under my supervision, directed and carried out the extensive research for this book. Michael graduated from Carleton University and Université d'Ottawa in Political Science. His advice, knowledge, and hard work were invaluable to me at every stage in the preparation of the manuscript. The author of a book such as this needs a key collaborator to talk to and plan with. Michael was just that person for me. Thanks so very much, Mike.

My thanks also to Dr. Luc Fortin, ex-professor at Université d'Ottawa and now carrying out research for the Library of Parliament. Luc helped me with the material and recommended Michael O'Neill as director of research.

To Erik Spicer, chief librarian, and his staff at the Library of Parliament goes my appreciation. Thanks also to Bruce Wise who worked with Michael O'Neill on the research.

My dear friend the late Hugh MacLennan gave me sound advice on substance as well as writing style, as did the late Frank Lowe of the former *Montreal Star* and *Weekend* magazine.

To my mother and high school and university teachers, such as the late Robert Speirs, Frank Scott and Ken Homer — how can I thank you enough for giving me a love for books and my mother tongue?

Thanks also go to Jonathan Williams, now residing in Ireland, for his editorial suggestions.

To Andi McInenly and Suzanne Sarda, my thanks for typing and re-typing the manuscript.

Thanks also to Jack Stoddart and all his associates, especially Angel Guerra and Donald G. Bastian, for having such confidence in my work.

Almost last but certainly not least, my editor, Alison Reid, who put up with my many eccentricities. In many ways, she was like a jockey who had to rein me in on the backstretch. Her sense of humour served both of us well. I am grateful, too, to Beverley Endersby and Doris Cowan for their important editorial contributions.

Authors invariably complain that writing can often be a lonely pursuit. That is so, but bringing a manuscript to completion is also a collaborative team effort. This has certainly been the case with me, and I am filled with a deep sense of gratitude and appreciation to so many good people.

1

THE NEED FOR REFORM

A few years ago, I was coming down in the elevator from my apartment in Ottawa, accompanied by an elderly lady who lived in the same building. She had a keen mind, and our short discussions usually concerned public affairs. That day, I asked her, "What do you think about democracy in Canada right now?" "I wouldn't know," she replied. "We haven't tried it yet."

One of the most important failures of our democratic system is in the way we select our party leaders. If the fundamental principle of parliamentary democracy is the notion that "the people" should have a say in how they will be governed and in what laws will be passed, surely the people should also have a say in the choice of the leaders of our political parties. Democracy demands no less. This principle is particularly true for Canada, where our prime minister exercises considerable power — far greater, for example, than that exercised by the president of the United States. The prime minister controls the party's policies and appoints people to hundreds of senior positions. The prime minister decides who will speak in cabinet and who will be listened to. In Canada, the tug of war between theory and practice in political life is nowhere better demonstrated than in the conflict between the ideals of democracy and how we live up to them when it comes to choosing the party leaders who will be eligible to become prime minister.

How do we select our party leaders in Canada? Do we have a say in choosing them? Why is it that we get leaders we don't want, and only *then*, when it is too late to do anything about it, cry bloody murder?

Both Mulroney and Chrétien were chosen by a totally unrepresentative élite, and their campaigns were floated on a sea of unreported dollars. The convention that chose McLaughlin never attempted to consult the grass roots in the first place. We should be ashamed of this national disgrace — a disgrace that sees teenagers and drunks bused to delegate-selection meetings in individual ridings, a disgrace that permits millions of campaign dollars to be raised and go unreported. When a leadership candidate must raise at least $2 million before "declaring," serious questions must be asked. It is a sad commentary on a great country and on its people.

At the next general election, we may get a choice. But will it be a real choice if no Liberals, Progressive Conservatives, or New Democrats at the grass-roots level have been consulted about the leader of their party? Will we be choosing the leader we want or only voting for the least undesirable among candidates whom we cannot comfortably respect? How will the Reform Party and the Bloc Québécois affect the outcome?

We are approaching a general election that could be a landmark — or could prove or solve nothing. How did we arrive at the present situation? How can we change things? How can we truly reform our leadership-selection process along democratic lines so that you and I can have our say? How can we get out of the mess we are in today? These questions involve basic democratic rights and freedoms.

THE NEED FOR REFORM

We get leaders we don't want because we didn't participate in choosing them. This situation is intolerable when the media focus our attention on our political party leaders to the near exclusion of cabinet ministers and back-benchers. All this media attention has not given us national heroes; rather, Canadians are disillusioned about the leaders who are placed before the public at election time. Canadians are annoyed at their inability to get the quality of leadership they want.

Most of us are only vaguely familiar with the way our leaders are selected. Even if you support a specific political party, you were probably not consulted, directly or indirectly, about your preference for that party's leader. Were you consulted about Brian Mulroney, Jean Chrétien, or Audrey McLaughlin? Our system doesn't have to leave voters alienated from the process.

Millions of Canadians during the past thirty years or so have watched our political parties select their leaders in huge, U.S.-style conventions. Many people wrongly believe that because large-scale leadership conventions are held in both Canada and the United States, our methods for electing party leaders are similar. In fact, the U.S. primary system permits individual citizens to vote and participate at the grassroots level. They have a chance to vote for the leader of their party at state primaries and caucuses long before the actual party convention is held. In Canada, our methods for selecting delegates to national leadership conventions are so haphazard and unregulated that our whole population is left with a sense of misgiving and disillusionment.

Let us be honest with ourselves: our individual and collective indifference has played no small role in this sorry state of affairs. The blame doesn't lie with Chrétien, Mulroney, or McLaughlin. They have played by the rules and won by the rules. Maybe, in fact, all of them would have reached their positions of leadership under a reformed process, but that possibility does not alter the issue.

If we are asked to vote for leaders we don't want at election time, leaders we never supported at an earlier stage, what kind of choice are we really being given? A true choice must be democratic; from its very outset, it must involve you and me.

Our leadership-selection process is crying out for reform. We need to explore some of the problems that attend the present process, look at how other countries choose their leaders, and recommend a direction for change.

I represented the rural Québec riding of Brome–Missisquoi, 75 per cent francophone, for eighteen years. It was a riding where I was able and obliged to get personally close to my constituents. Their concerns about the leadership crisis have troubled me. Now I see their frustration mirrored across the country, and I realize that it is time for us to change our process of leadership selection.

My own disillusionment with the way we choose our leaders began with the conventions that nominated John Diefenbaker and Lester Pearson as party leaders. Those conventions demonstrated a general apathy regarding public affairs and our political institutions. Participation at these two Ottawa conventions was casual and unenthusiastic. The conventions had more value as publicity vehicles for the political parties than as forums for the expression of democratic choice.

The Progressive Conservative leadership-nominating convention was held at the Ottawa Coliseum on December 14, 1956. George Drew had retired for reasons of ill health, and a successor had to be named. Twenty-two years in opposition had drained the enthusiasm of party workers. There is a time-worn axiom in politics that governments too long in power grow stale and arrogant. What is less obvious but equally serious is that parties too long in opposition become equally stale and oppose lamely. Even the three major contenders — John Diefenbaker, Donald Fleming, and E. Davie Fulton — were running dry and unexciting campaigns. In Brome–Missisquoi, in the late fall of 1956, there were no delegates selected to attend the Ottawa convention. Senior Progressive Conservative workers seemed indifferent to the event. Such was the case in ridings throughout Canada.

At the convention, delegates were registered in a haphazard way. They did not have to prove that they were Progressive Conservative party members. Anybody who could afford the trip to Ottawa became, in effect, a delegate. Only two people from Brome–Missisquoi made the journey. The rest of our slate was filled with substitutes from other parts of the province. This practice was so common that the term "blow-in delegate" was coined to describe a substitute who was appointed to fill a spot originally allocated to an elected riding representative. Diefenbaker emerged as the easy victor, winning on the first ballot with 774 votes to 393 for Fleming and 117 for Fulton. We cannot be sure whether this result reflected the will or the indifference of the party membership as a whole.

In January 1958, the Liberals named Lester Pearson to head the party. The Grits' selection of a leader was even less dependent on the will of the Canadian public than the Tory choice had been. Pearson was chosen by the party generals. St. Laurent selected Pearson, and that endorsement effectively ended the chances of Pearson's main opponent, the hapless Paul Martin. The Liberal convention was packed with *ex officio* delegates and delegates at large to ensure the coronation of the bow-tied wonder from External Affairs.

The nomination of Pearson was in line with recent Liberal Party tradition. Until the time of Laurier, the Liberal Party caucus had chosen their leader. Interestingly, their leaders have all come from central Canada and have emerged through a kind of apostolic succession. Laurier laid his hands on King; King laid his hands on St. Laurent; St. Laurent laid his hands on Pearson; Pearson laid his hands on Trudeau; and Trudeau laid his hands on nobody. The succession was not left open to popular choice. If the foot-soldiers in the Liberal party wanted Jean Chrétien in 1984, they didn't have a chance of getting their wish. Maybe their hearts were with Chrétien, but the generals wanted Turner and got him. The grass roots were ignored.

When I entered the political process in 1957, I found it hard to believe that in a so-called democratic country, we selected our leaders in such a disorganized way. Nothing has improved. It seems incredible to me that some thirty years later, there is such chaos in all party ranks over the selection of leaders. In many ways, the situation is worse now than it was in 1956. The chickens have come home to roost. We can no longer ignore the need for reform.

As a member of Parliament, I have watched the rise of six prime ministers and the evolution of Canada's third-largest party, the New Democratic Party. In all my political experience, a riding meeting in 1983 was easily the saddest event for me.

Delegates were to be chosen from my riding of Brome–Missisquoi to attend the PC leadership convention to be held that June, in Ottawa. Clark and Mulroney were the principal contenders. The local party executive, under the direction of its president, Louis Cournoyer, had held a number of preparatory meetings. Our association membership was approximately one thousand, and only card-carrying members in good standing could vote at the delegate-selection meeting. I had to explain this principle, as the idea of membership cards had never been accepted by the local association, and none of its members possessed a card. This time, the requirement for membership cards was handed down by the party's National Executive. This time, things would be different, and I persuaded Cournoyer and the rest of the executive of the necessity to get out and sell membership cards to the association members on our lists — lists that had been built up over the previous twenty-five years. They did a reasonably good job and sold about four hundred cards, with no effort whatsoever to influence individual party members in favour of one candidate or another. I was publicly supporting Clark, but my hope for the meeting was to see concerned party workers sent to Ottawa to weigh the candidates thoughtfully and to vote for their considered choice as the best leader. The party executive knew that the Mulroney organization was active in the riding. They felt that selling four hundred membership cards to established party supporters would be enough to offset any practices that might undermine the democratic intent of the process.

Brian Mulroney had a lot of friends in the riding who had summer residences there, but whose roots were mainly in Montréal or elsewhere. None of them had ever worked in the local association or in local elections. Michel Cogger, now a senator, directed the campaign for Mulroney in Brome–Missisquoi with what seemed limitless funds.

It was a cool day in the early spring of 1983 when I drove from Ottawa to Cowansville with Professor Luc Fortin of the University of Ottawa. The meeting was to be held at the local community centre.

As Fortin and I drove into the parking area of the centre, my heart sank. Apart from the two hundred or so cars one expects at such events, there were also about twenty yellow school buses. I had heard of the busing in of drunks and schoolchildren by Mulroney forces on the Island of Montréal, but I had not anticipated such a large-scale operation in my old rural riding, the one riding in the province of Québec that had remained constant and faithful to the PC cause during thick and thin over the previous twenty-five years. In the hall, I took a seat alongside Louis Cournoyer. Sitting quietly to my left were four hundred of our regular workers and organizers, long-time members of the association. They had come from every corner of the riding, and I knew each one of them by name. The thousand or so remaining participants were largely screaming adolescents, with the exception of the Mulroney operatives, who looked glamorous enough to have just left a nearby cocktail party. I had never before seen such richly dressed and haughty people at a political rally in that area. The great majority were the children of well-to-do Montréalers, mostly weekenders from the Brome Lake area. This operation probably constituted a first exposure to public affairs for most of them. The Mulroney slate of delegates was circulated. It took Chairman Cournoyer some time to establish order as the screaming young people continued to chant, "Brian! Brian! Brian!" In view of my long involvement in the riding and the party, Cournoyer asked me to address the meeting. I was loudly booed for several solid minutes, the first time I had ever experienced that reaction from people in my own party in all my political career. The booing reached a crescendo as I told the crowd that while it was no secret which leadership candidate I supported, I had in no way attempted to influence others in the association, and that included Cournoyer himself. The younger participants continued to boo and hiss. Perhaps because of their cynical introduction into the political process, they found it hard to believe that there were still people who care more about how the game is played than about winning. I noted that while Cournoyer had been the association's president for twenty-five years and had fought alongside me during ten federal elections, I had no idea how Louis would vote.

THE NEED FOR REFORM

Because of his services to the party, I had hoped that those present would unanimously name him a delegate to the convention. I was dreaming. The boos increased. Cournoyer was not selected as a delegate, and the Mulroney slate was voted in.

In the parking lot, Mulroney's people shouted insults at me. The old-time members filed out of the hall in funereal fashion. Such short-term expediency meant long-term trouble. Few of the Mulroney contingent at this meeting are members of the association today. Many of them threw away their membership cards in the parking lot after the vote. Gabrielle Bertrand, the current MP for Brome–Missisquoi, spends much of her time buoying up the riding association that was so bruised by this operation. Cournoyer quit the association, as did many other members. Mulroney sent emissaries to appease him. The new leader even wished to present him with some sort of plaque in recognition of his past services when he next visited the riding. He had seriously underestimated the pride and self-esteem of people like Cournoyer. The honours were not accepted. The damage to the party's unity was not to be so easily repaired.

Later in the day, after the delegate-selection meeting, I returned to my home. Journalists telephoned for interviews. One caller asked how I felt now that I was no longer the "boss" of the PC Association in Brome–Missisquoi. I told him I had never been the boss, but he didn't seem to understand.

The significance of this story lies not in the fate of one vote in one riding, but in the way people with influence and money can cut their own path to positions of political power. It is about the subverting of democracy. What happened in my riding happens in many ridings, with minor variants. We need to consider the process and regain our right of democratic choice. We need to regain our respect for our leaders by selecting leaders who have earned our respect.

PART ONE

HOW WE NOMINATE PARTY CANDIDATES

2

GETTING GRASS-ROOTS EXPERIENCE

"GOOD LUCK ON YOUR WAY TO PARLIAMENT HILL"

"Good luck on your way to Parliament Hill" were the first words of encouragement I received; they appeared in my high-school graduation magazine in the spring of 1946. To be a member of Parliament, representing thousands of people in the national legislature, was my boyhood dream. At first, I had wanted to be a doctor, and a little later, I yearned to be a medical missionary, but a high-school visit to Ottawa gave me a new resolve. My family and friends never held politicians in high esteem, so I received little outside encouragement, except for the odd reference to the lofty ideals of public service, which did not necessarily include the pursuit of elective office.

In 1958, at the age of twenty-nine, I was sworn in to the House of Commons as the new member for Brome–Missisquoi, a constituency in Québec's Eastern Townships, between Montréal and Sherbrooke. At that time, the riding was approximately 70 per cent French-speaking. Since my mother tongue was English, I considered it a great honour and responsibility to represent such an electorate. Between

1957 and 1980, I stood as a candidate in ten federal elections, and most of my years in the House were spent on the opposition benches. There were frustrations, but my advice to anyone contemplating public service in the House of Commons is "Give it a try." Young people ask me when is the right time for them to stand. The truth is that there never really is a right time. Each individual intuitively knows when he or she should take the plunge. It is a personal decision.

Serving in the House is a rewarding experience, with endless satisfactions. It requires sacrifices, but so does all worthwhile work. The hours are long and the problems sometimes seem insoluble, but anybody holding a seat in the Commons who is willing to work hard is given unbounded scope to get things done. With a little creative imagination, the life of a parliamentarian becomes a fascinating and, in John Buchan's words, an "honourable adventure."

My baptism of fire involving the so-called democratic process took place at the grass-roots level. In the spring of 1956 — a vintage year for me — I witnessed the nomination of the Union Nationale candidate for Brome County in Québec. Nothing resembling democratic procedures took place. High drama and farce were the order of the day. Later, in December of the same year, John Diefenbaker was nominated as leader for the Progressive Conservative Party. I witnessed the Ottawa convention in total disbelief. The slack way in which Dief was named abrogated all the fundamental rules we could expect for "free and open conventions." These two events in 1956 surely affected my youthful ideals and enthusiasm. At any rate, my rose-coloured glasses were gone.

When I was a boy, I revered a good member of Parliament just as Wayne Gretzky hero-worshipped Gordie Howe. (When, in 1977, my peers and *Canadian Magazine* named me one of Canada's ten best MPs, my pride and happiness were unsurpassed. It was like hitting over 300 in baseball, or being named to an all-star team.) For me, the House of Commons was and is "the highest forum in the land." I also assumed that getting a party nomination involved fundamental democratic procedures. I often asked myself, as many young people may be asking today, "How do you go about getting nominated? What's involved?" Only too soon, I would find out.

On October 1, 1948, a few days after my father's death, I was staying with my sister and brother-in-law at the family farm, "Meadowlands," in Knowlton, when we heard of the sudden death of Jon Robinson, the provincial member for Brome and the minister of Mines in the Duplessis cabinet. The premier prevailed on Warwick Fox, a pulp-and-paper executive, to stand for the Union Nationale in the by-election, and he won the seat. During his years in the legislature, Fox never really took to active political life and he delegated much of his constituency work to two residents of Brome County, Jim Jolley and Eddie Persons. Jolley, a representative for Beattie Brothers Farm Equipment, eventually became Fox's riding secretary, a position that enabled him to build up considerable standing in the constituency. Fox delegated many of his riding duties to Eddie Persons, a contractor from the town of Sweetsburg, who was heavily involved in the building of roads and bridges. During Fox's term of office, the local power and influence of Jolley and Persons grew simultaneously.

By the time Maurice Duplessis called the June 1956 provincial election, Fox announced that he intended to resign, and I was determined to test these turbulent waters by helping to organize for the party in Brome County. A year earlier, I had been admitted to the Québec bar and was president and chief executive officer of the Montreal Lumber Company. I had managed to get control of the company with help from the bank. Together with an industrious staff, I succeeded in putting the firm in a healthy market position.

Although I worked in Montréal, my roots were still in Brome County, and on most weekends I would visit my sister at the family farm. The farm was originally owned by the Honourable Sidney Fisher, who had served for fifteen years as minister of Agriculture under Sir Wilfrid Laurier. Fisher lived next door, at Alva House, and it was here that Laurier held one of his last strategy meetings in late November 1918, with half a dozen leaders of the Liberal Party. Brome County legend attributes a good story to Fisher. During his last campaign he declared, "I have the election in my pocket." He then went on to lose by one vote.

The family farm served as a base for my campaign during 1957. I had talked a lot about politics over the years and had been writing political reviews for various Montréal newspapers. My friends told me that the time had now come to put up or shut up, but I did not need much persuading. Many years before, I had become fascinated by the political process.

One Friday evening in mid-April 1956, I was passing through Sweetsburg, and I stopped for a coffee at Bill's Diner. I went to a pay phone downstairs and rang Jean-Jacques Bertrand, the local provincial member for Missisquoi, who, in October 1968, would succeed Daniel Johnson as Québec premier. I wanted to help Bertrand in his re-election bid, and we arranged to meet the following morning in his law office. His provincial riding took in a large part of my future federal constituency and was a good 80 per cent French-speaking.

Bertrand was extremely gracious and accepted my offer of help, but suggested that I concentrate on Brome County, where the Union Nationale was expecting a tough fight. His worries turned out to be justified.

Although I had studied French, I wanted grass-roots experience in a francophone milieu. After completing high school at Lower Canada College in Montreal, I went off to Mount Allison University in New Brunswick, and later studied law at McGill. It was when I was at the Montreal Lumber Company that my friend Bunty Roy suggested that I meet Jeannine McLay, an elderly lady who lived downtown, to see if she could help me brush up on my French. Jeannine, a Belgian national who had married a doctor from Hamilton, was a tough taskmaster. For two years, we had lunch three times a week. I prepared lessons, took dictation, went to French plays, read *Le Devoir*, and watched the television news in French. Jeannine and I really hit it off. During the summer breaks, I used to write her three letters a week. She would send them back corrected, with a covering letter. Before long, she made an earnest twenty-four-year-old functionally bilingual. A new world was opened to me.

As soon as Fox announced his retirement, Jolley and Persons both started actively seeking the Union Nationale nomination. Duplessis made it clear that because of possible political conflict, he did not want a road contractor to run, but Persons refused to back down. The Union Nationale, founded by Duplessis in Sherbrooke in 1935, was a loose coalition of dissident Conservatives and Liberals. Before long, the Liberals left the coalition, and the party evolved into a hard-core nationalist and conservative force.

The party convention was slated for April 26, 1956, in the Knowlton High School. Well over a thousand people, including hundreds of Liberals, crowded into the hall to witness the Persons–Jolley duel. Much animosity existed between the rivals, so Duplessis, anticipating a fiery evening, sent his minister of Colonization, Joseph D. Bégin, to preside over the balloting. Open and democratic conventions were not common in the Union Nationale; more often than not, Duplessis simply named the local candidate. Bégin's unease was glaringly apparent from the moment he arrived. Successive glances at his wristwatch gave the audience the distinct impression that he had not set aside too much time for the proceedings.

The fun started when Jolley presented Bégin with his official list of 104 delegates. Then Persons approached the platform and handed Bégin *his* list of 104 delegates. The two lists of names were totally different. Bégin, not unnaturally, was confused, but he soon hit upon an ingenious procedure, which to him had all the hallmarks of true local democracy. Not knowing any of the county's residents by name, he demonstrated his impartiality by ignoring both lists. The local citizenry were uncharacteristically in awe of the impatient, limousine-driven minister. Here was his ruse: there were (for example) five polling divisions for Knowlton and fifteen voting delegates. Bégin asked everybody from the town to stand up. Then he called out, "You in the red shirt; you in the blue suit; you in the green dress," until he had selected fifteen people. He did this town by town, municipality by municipality, until he had his slate of delegates. The only trouble was that Bégin unwittingly picked a number of solid Liberals, much to the horror of the local Tory old-timers and to the pleasure of the Liberals in the hall. However, he received assurances from Persons and Jolley that they would accept the delegates' verdict and that the loser would openly and diligently support the victor. When Bégin announced the results of the ballot, Jolley had squeaked through by three votes. The usual arm-raising of the winner by the vanquished never took place. Persons announced that he would spend the cost of a bulldozer to beat Jolley on election day — a threat that turned out to be pretty close to the truth.

During the ensuing campaign, Jolley became caught up in local organizational difficulties — especially in mending his fences with Persons's supporters — and he did not get out to meet the people. As I criss-crossed the county, canvassing, it was obvious to me that the Union Nationale was divided. Persons was not to be tamed, and his internecine fight with Jolley carried on right up to the day of the vote. Few gave the Liberal candidate, Glen Brown, any chance of winning. I acted as chairman for most of Jolley's public meetings. The big guns came down from Québec City to lend a hand. One Friday evening, halfway through the campaign, Jean-Jacques Bertrand and Daniel Johnson both turned up to address the same meeting.

On the night before election day, Jolley staged a huge motorcade parade around Knowlton and then held a mass outdoor rally in front of the high school. After looking out at the crowd, he turned to me and said, "Heward, the election is in the bag." I was reminded of the overconfident Sidney Fisher and his one-vote loss. Besides, the crowd was not at all friendly. Big crowds and a certain *bonhomie* all too often precede a political burial as much as they do a political victory. The next day, Glen Brown, a history teacher at the local high school and an ex-football player, defeated Jolley, with 3,274 votes to Jolley's 3,029.

The scene was set for the federal election, and my work for the federal Progressive Conservative party was to begin. It was plain that Québec Conservatives were in trouble. The reported remark of the Tory national leader, George Drew, when he was premier of Ontario, that family allowances were a sop to Quebeckers with large families, had been well publicized by the Grits. Also, Louis St. Laurent had ancestral roots in Compton, Québec, just a few miles from the eastern extremities of Brome–Missisquoi. As a youth, the prime minister had spoken French to his father and English to his mother, so he was fluently bilingual; he was generally regarded as a rather courtly and honourable gentleman.

Since Brome–Missisquoi is in the heart of the Eastern Townships, the prime minister's favourite-son status made things harder for Progressive Conservatives. In the 1953 election, the Tory party had lost all of the constituency's 110 polling divisions except one, winning barely a quarter of the popular vote. The local party had no identifiable organization.

At this time, I began to piece together names of active workers to build up a master list that would be ready for a nominating convention. Things were a lot harder in Missisquoi County. Jean-Jacques Bertrand advised me to go to a nearby town to talk to the local crown attorney, Maurice Archambault, who had done organizational work for Bertrand. Archambault was also a personal friend of Bertrand's and Daniel Johnson's, and had attended university with them and Jean Drapeau, who was soon to become mayor of Montréal. The attorney was reserved and seemed reluctant to hand over copies of his organizational lists to an eager young turk. Every ounce of persuasion and diplomacy I could muster was to no avail, and I left Archambault's office empty-handed.

The weeks passed and I put thousands of miles on my car over the back roads, calling on party militants to try to winkle out every possible Conservative supporter.

In a last-ditch stand to build up a constituency workers' list, I visited party headquarters on Ottawa's Laurier Avenue, early in the new year of 1957. Flora MacDonald and Dalton Camp were working there at the time. All that could be found in the Brome–Missisquoi file was a telegram from George Drew, congratulating our sacrificial-lamb candidate for carrying the party banner during the previous election

I had exhausted every possibility of building up an extensive list of party members, but the time for decision had arrived. To have a ghost of a chance of winning the seat, a candidate needed at least six months to canvass every part of the riding, and to get known and build up an organization. There was not even a formal riding executive. Who would organize and call a convention? In most Québec ridings, the same sorry state of affairs existed. When the Liberals announced an election, weeks would go by before the Tories named their candidates from party headquarters. They did not call local conventions, but, at the eleventh hour, boasted that a great national party had a full slate of candidates from coast to coast. It was pathetic.

Using the list I had put together after visiting the parishes and municipalities in my riding and seeking out party supporters, I wrote a letter to local party workers, stating my intention to run at a properly organized convention, which I said should be summoned soon. Subsequently, I arranged to have another letter sent out under the signature of local party officials, announcing that a convention would be held in Cowansville on February 5, 1957.

It became clear to me that I would have to be the prime mover in organizing the convention, albeit with incomplete lists. The inadequacy of these lists was only too evident as I entered the convention hall. Many delegates still regarded me as an outsider. Scores of older Conservative supporters clustered around the hall's entrance; they had seen and read the newspaper ads announcing the meeting, but had not received written invitations. But did this make them any less a Blue than their neighbour? I arranged for somebody to write out their names, addresses, and phone numbers; they were to be visited soon after the convention by me or whoever was the party's official candidate. On the night of the convention, they were furious.

The convention itself was high drama. Léon Balcer, Progressive Conservative MP for Trois-Rivières, presided over the proceedings. Brome County made up less than a third of the riding's population, but was far better represented at the meeting. One after another, the delegates from outside Brome County got up and said that the convention would be postponed until fairer representation from Missisquoi County could be summoned. Unfortunately, there were some significant undertones here, since Missisquoi County was much more heavily French-speaking than Brome. Balcer said that he sympathized, but his province-wide responsibilities meant that he could not return to the riding before election day. History would repeat itself, Balcer said: the candidate would be named on the eve of the vote, only to be humiliated by the big Liberal machine.

I sat nervously in the crowd, knowing that a postponement would mean certain defeat at the polls for me or any other candidate because there would be insufficient time to mount a proper campaign. To my horror, a friend from the 1956 provincial campaign, Gaétan Mireault, soon to become my Man Friday, stood up and proposed that the convention be deferred. He was sitting directly in front of me. I tapped him discreetly on the shoulder, and he pulled back a bit. Nevertheless, bedlam broke out in the hall. Balcer had lost control of the meeting, so he called for a recess. During the break, he convened a private caucus of the dissident Missisquoi supporters. The parleying seemed interminable, and I could hear raised voices. At one point, I felt that it was a lost cause, but Balcer carried a lot of weight in the party and eventually convinced the reluctant Missisquoi County workers not to seek a postponement. It was not an auspicious beginning.

Balcer took the stand and called for nominations from the floor. Fabie Shaw from Knowlton placed my name in nomination. As she extolled my virtues, somebody yelled out, "Hell, we don't want a saint for a candidate!" Maj.-Gen. Basil Price, a friend of my father's, seconded the nomination (Doug Abbott, St. Laurent's minister of Finance, had beaten

Price by sixty-nine votes in the 1945 general election in St. Antoine–Westmount). My nomination was secure and went unopposed. Tory nominations were not sought-after prizes in Québec in the winter of 1957. At the age of twenty-eight, I was the fully fledged candidate for the Progressive Conservative party in Brome–Missisquoi. The shaky beginning was over.

Democracy is an ideal; we should try giving it a chance in Canada. Today, scores of members of Parliament on both sides of the House of Commons are sitting without having been chosen by open and democratic constituency conventions. Until all candidates are named by open conventions, for all practical purposes, we shall continue to make a mockery of democratic principles.

My nominating convention was imperfect in terms of "democratic procedure." It was, nevertheless, a vast improvement over past practices in the riding when the national office in Ottawa merely named a sacrificial-lamb candidate at the last moment before an election.

3

TRANSITION TO POWER

At the beginning of September, Diefenbaker asked me to see him in his East Block offices. When I arrived, he was in a furious mood. He had just offered Roland Michener the speakership of the House, but the member for St. Paul's fervently wished to be named minister of External Affairs. This news had been leaked to the press, and Diefenbaker had gone into a tailspin. In those days, the prime minister nominated the future speaker after consultation with the leaders of the opposition parties. Such nominations were habitually rubber-stamped by the full membership of the House. The current speaker, the Honourable John Fraser, was the first to hold this office on the basis of a secret vote by the total membership of the House. In this instance, democracy has been well served.

While the House was in session in Ottawa, my organizers in Brome–Missisquoi all felt that another general election was imminent, and that we could not maintain our precarious minority situation. The Gallup poll continued to bring us good news, and Dief had the wind in his sails. When Louis St. Laurent announced his retirement in early September, even the Québec picture brightened for the Tories.

As the fall approached, it became clear that a convention should be called to choose a candidate for Brome–Missisquoi. When the winds of change blow for the better for a political party, all kinds of potential candidates start to creep out of the woodwork. My organization was ad hoc and piecemeal. While I had recruited and organized about a thousand workers for the June 1957 election, there was no formal distinction between the party organization and the association. The former is responsible essentially for getting out the vote on election day. While there is generally and ideally one campaign manager, the candidate usually controls and directs the organization during and between elections. Most people who help in the organization are also members of the party association, but the latter is the permanent party presence in the constituency and comes under the aegis of the elected president and the riding executive. Organization and association functions frequently overlap and are inevitably duplicated. Some people strongly prefer organizational work, which centres on election activity, while others are more disposed to association activities, such as policy forums. Both are essential, but the party that recognizes the fundamental difference between the association and the party organization has a tremendous advantage. My party's failure to understand such a distinction, especially in Québec, largely contributed to our poor showing before September 4, 1984.

It was tempting to opt for short-cut expediency. I knew that the thousand or so workers would be loyal to me. Why not just call a convention that could nominate a candidate? To do so would have been easy and probably would have guaranteed my nomination, but it would have been wrong. At any rate, Senator Alistair Grosart, the party's national campaign director, had other ideas. Nominating conventions were to be convened by an association executive properly elected by the party faithful. Three delegates and two alternates were to be named by party members in each polling division. I rather think this rule was not evenly applied in all Québec ridings because of the party's woefully weak position in the province. However, it was to be applied in Brome–Missisquoi, and I had to live with that fact. As it turned out, the election of a party executive in the riding for the first time in living memory, and the eventual nomination of poll delegates and alternates for the convention, turned out to be key factors in democratizing our party and enabled me to organize and hold the seat for a long time.

The naming of a democratically elected riding executive and the drawing up of a constitution and rules to ensure that poll delegates were openly elected proved to be invaluable experience and were, as already mentioned, central factors in my successive re-elections. The process guaranteed that I would be in constant touch with grass-roots sentiments, which I, in turn, could translate to the party leadership in Ottawa.

Later in September 1957, I saw Maurice Archambault in his legal offices in Farnham. He invited me back to his home for a long cross-examination of my intentions, over many black coffees sweetened with large quantities of cognac. It soon dawned on me what Archambault had in mind; on October 4, he announced his candidacy for the Conservative nomination for Brome–Missisquoi. I knew that he would gather support from his home town of Farnham and its environs, where there was a pronounced nationalist sentiment in favour of a francophone nominee, which in many ways was understandable.

On November 5, I announced my own candidacy, but an association executive still had not been elected. Jean-Jacques Bertrand's brother-in-law, Fernand Giroux, was a tireless worker and an excellent organizer for my cause, and Louis Cournoyer headed a slate of executive nominees who were behind me. The big test came at Cowansville on November

14, in a large secondary-school basement. Well over a thousand people turned up and, by a handsome margin, elected Cournoyer as association president. We had jumped a big hurdle, but Archambault refused to withdraw from the race, even though an executive obviously favourable to my candidacy had been elected.

The newly elected executive met within a few days and set December 19 as the convention date. Once more, Léon Balcer was to preside. The night was extremely stormy, with very icy roads. Some people had as much as a fifty-mile drive to Cowansville, but that did not prevent a record turnout of close to two thousand. After the speeches, the roll-call of delegates was read. Amazingly, not a single delegate failed to turn up. The result was 250 votes for me and 69 for Archambault, with two spoiled ballots. After the announcement, Balcer turned to me and muttered, "Sixty-nine isn't enough for a judgeship." Later on I would find out the significance of his remark.

It seems inexplicable that more than twenty-five years later, there is such chaos in the Conservative, Liberal, and NDP ranks over the naming of candidates at riding conventions. If there was such a thing as grass-roots democracy within local party organizations, how could Pierre Trudeau, in 1965, have been imposed from the top on the Mount Royal Liberal Association when there were so many other deserving and better candidates who had paid their dues? And how else to explain the nomination of Trudeau's friend, Jim Coutts, in Spadina? Sometimes my party was just as bad.

Bob Stanfield became wedded to the lieutenancy principle in Québec — in which one party strongman is virtually a deputy prime minister, or leader, for Québec — first choosing Marcel Faribeault, the distinguished head of Les Trusts Généraux, in the 1968 general election, and subsequently Claude Wagner, as his Québec leader. For Faribeault, the party hierarchy in Québec inexplicably picked the working-class riding of Gamelin in the east end of Montréal. During the campaign, Faribeault was driven by taxi to shake hands with some dock workers in his newly chosen constituency. The urbane financier could not stand the hand-shaking routine. On election day, he was trounced at the polls.

Then there was the débâcle in 1982 in Toronto–Greenwood, a former Toronto riding, when Peter Worthington upset the applecart for the Conservatives and ran as an independent, denying the party an expected by-election victory. J. Patrick Boyer, then a Toronto lawyer, now a member of Parliament for Etobicoke–Lakeshore, presided over the voting-credential certification committee — a committee charged with ascertaining that those voting did, in fact, have the right to vote — for the party candidate in the Toronto–Greenwood by-election. After reading his report, I realized that he must have felt like a judge making rulings where there were no regulations and no precedents, since the report underlined that the only law was the law of the jungle.

Typical of nomination battles before the 1988 elections was the contest in Mississauga, Ontario, that saw insurance broker Arminde Silva lose by seventy-one votes to Albina Guarnieri, former press secretary to Toronto Mayor Art Eggleton and to the Ontario Liberal leader. This ugly, chaotic nomination fight, like so many in the Metro Toronto area, made a farce of democracy, reported the *Globe and Mail* on July 14, 1988. Hardened political veterans were horrified by the tactics used — tactics that saw partisans buying thousands of dollars' worth of membership cards, "stuffing ballot boxes and frequently helping people to vote two or three times." Stevie Cameron reported, "If this is democracy, it's time to try something else." Cameron went on to repeat, "The Liberals are paying a high price for democracy Toronto style."

On August 17, 1988, William Johnson of the Montréal *Gazette* followed up with an equally devastating column, relating to the Québec scene. His column, entitled, "Democracy is withering at grass roots," constituted a hard-hitting indictment of current nominating practices. His article criticized the undemocratic procedure that permits a party to name a candidate without a nomination endorsement by local party members. Local citizens are deprived of a voice in the nomination process. A weakly controlled nomination meeting can result in a candidate's being imposed on the whole community. What is democratic about that?

Johnson ended his article by outlining certain basic rules that should be followed at nomination conventions:

- All members eligible to vote at nominations should be able to vote in a general election. That is, they should be at least eighteen years old, Canadian citizens, and residents of the riding.
- Candidates should be required to disclose the source and use of all money spent on a nomination bid for examination by the party, in an audited report. Thus, it will be clear who donated money and how it was used.
- The party must have the staff and ability to adhere to the rules and apply them consistently and without bias.
- Voters must have been members of their party for at least twelve months in order to establish their conviction and to prevent abuses.
- There must be strict photo identification in order to vote.

The question must be asked: does the simple possession of a party membership card guarantee that its holder is a bona fide party supporter? Conversely, does the declaration of party support by a resident of the riding automatically entitle him or her to a membership card? As it is, if rules and regulations are not standardized and enforced when candidates are nominated by card-carrying party members in a large hall, the whole thing becomes a sham. Voting for the party nominee resembles voting for a carnival queen, when the group that sells the most tickets for the princess of their choice wins the day. It is arguable that this method brings new blood into the party ranks, but the resulting chaos and inevitable resentment, when hundreds of strangers and new faces are bussed in to party meetings, more than offset this advantage.

At the constituency level, the alternative to having card-carrying party members choose the nominee is to adopt a system of three delegates and two alternates for each polling division, chosen by party workers. If this is not done, or if the rules governing party membership cards stay as slack, we shall continue to treat democratic principles frivolously.

Diefenbaker was a House of Commons man and a populist at heart. Even in Québec, he did everything possible to make sure that nomination meetings were openly and democratically held. In a letter addressed to me just after the first session of the 1958 Parliament, Diefenbaker wrote:

> As a party, we have much to be proud of, but we must, at all costs, guard against over-confidence, particularly in the matter of constituency organization. In many parts of the country, the organizations which carried us through the elections of 1957 and 1958 are comparatively new and much remains to be done in consolidating the ground gained. I have asked our National Headquarters to undertake (in cooperation with our members, constituency presidents and former candidates) a complete check of the status of the organization in all 265 constituencies. The objective for the period between now and the opening of the next session is the establishment of a broadly based, representa-

tive Federal Conservative Association in every constituency in Canada. By this I mean an association:

a) which will invite into its membership all who may wish to associate themselves with the future of the party
b) which will have an up-to-date written constitution
c) which will have a fully elected executive
d) which will hold regular meetings of both the executive and the association.

For years, Diefenbaker had been kicked around by the party élite, and he was sensitive to democratizing procedures at the constituency level. Thirty-two years have passed since I received the letter on constituency organization from Diefenbaker, and today things haven't really changed at all. The incomprehensible rule that the leader must sign nomination papers still exists. It gives him or her virtual veto power over the men or women chosen by members of the constituency association.

At the annual meeting of the Progressive Conservative Party in August 1989, I moved an amendment to the rule that requires the leader's signature on nomination papers, thus eliminating his power of veto over the wishes of the constituency association. The motion to pass this amendment was defeated.

Before the September 1984 general election, both John Turner and Brian Mulroney named scores of candidates across Canada to run in specific ridings. This practice was particularly pronounced in Québec. Once the leader's wishes became known, nomination meetings were summarily set aside. Many of these Conservative candidates were swept in on their leader's coat-tails. Their ability to keep the party informed of local concerns would subsequently be severely compromised. Allowing our leaders to hand-pick candidates bestows on them far too much power. Mulroney must truly build from the bottom up, especially in Québec.

If every member of Parliament were asked the question "Were you nominated by an open-ended democratic convention in your constituency?" the answer would invariably be a resounding yes. A call to the headquarters of all three national parties, asking if party nominees are required to submit themselves to open-ended democratic conventions, would elicit the same answer. In 1985, at the December annual meeting of my party in Montréal, I proposed a motion to the effect that such a convention process be mandatory. It was adopted, but, as is true of so many rules and ordinances, measures enforcing them are often weak or non-existent. The only effective remedy is an alert and active party membership in each riding, where the individual takes seriously his or her responsibility. What constitutes a democratic and open nominating convention? This question reminds me of a similar one: "When is a medical check-up deemed complete and proper?" The doctor could take one look at the patient and say that he or she looks fine, then end the check-up. At the other end of the spectrum is a long list of requirements similar to, among other things, taking blood pressure and temperature; examining ears, nose, and throat; monitoring heart beat and breathing, etc. And so it goes with party conventions — ranging from half a dozen people in a room to a convention called under the rules of the constituency association's constitution — adopted openly by the party membership and requiring proper notice over a reasonable period of time. Party élites are adept at avoiding such inconveniences.

A case in point was the nomination of Madame Jean-Jacques Bertrand in my old riding of Brome–Missisquoi before the September 1984 federal election. For some time, it was thought that the leader, Brian Mulroney, would run in the riding, but this plan was cast aside at the last moment. Madame Bertrand was Mulroney's personal choice. She was and is my friend, and when I was informed of Mulroney's intention by phone, I offered my support for her candidacy, while insisting on an open and democratic convention. That, however, seemed to be impossible as the leader wanted to announce her nomination in a few days. The association president, Gilles Mercure, called a meeting of the executive at Cowansville without delay. During the meeting, Mercure phoned me to say that Michel Cogger was present and that he had informed the executive that I told him I felt it was all right, under the circumstances, to waive the requirement for a convention. Such was not the case, and I relayed this information to Mercure in no uncertain terms. Madame Bertrand was duly named at the executive meeting, and so it goes.

In the ensuing years, when, most of the time, I was one of two members from Québec in the opposition, it was tempting to short-cut democratic procedures requiring a free and open convention. My party was weak and virtually non-existent in Québec — and, at each election, some took it for granted I would be the party standard-bearer in my riding. I was, but always on the condition that convention requirements were met. When a party is weak in a riding, or when a strong sitting member is coming up for re-election, it is easy to say, "Let's forget the convention." After all, it takes time and trouble to organize such an event. There is no fast-fix miracle cure. Freedom and democracy require the time and trouble of an eternally vigilant citizenry taking its responsibilities seriously. We must make sure candidates for a seat in the House are nominated by a representative and broad base of their constituents acting openly and freely. Surely that is not too much to ask.

Part Two

How We Nominate Party Leaders

4

LOOKING BACK

Canada is a comparatively young nation with regard to the development of national political institutions. We have borrowed our political traditions rather than developing our own. This fact is particularly evident in the manner in which we have selected our political party leaders over the years. In the early period of our nationhood, our political party leaders were chosen according to the traditions of the British political parties. By the 1990s, we had added American-style conventions. Soon we may be ready to make our own innovations.

LEADERSHIP SELECTION, 1850 TO 1920

In the years immediately preceding Confederation, there were only two organized and active political parties with any substantial following — the Reform Party led by George Brown and the Conservative Party led by John A. Macdonald. The unity of the parties came largely because they represented a clique of people with similar ideas, and neither Brown nor Macdonald was a party leader in the sense in which we now understand that role. Rather, each was the spokesman for his respective party, but had little power beyond this role. The leader rarely provided policy direction;

party policy was typically a matter of consensus among people who were of the same mind on most issues. The notion of party membership was also very different then from what it is today. The party was a very exclusive club, membership in which was reserved for a small group of people comprising the economically powerful élite or expatriate British upper class.

Policy decisions and the nominations for legislative elections were made at small meetings of the membership, numbering, at most, a few hundred. These meetings, often referred to as conventions, were usually held in English Canada at varying intervals. In 1849, for example, the Conservative Party held two such meetings, one in Kingston and one in Toronto. These meetings rarely lasted more than a day and would be considered informal by today's standards. The issue of leadership was not raised, although, in 1867, the Reform party met to endorse a resolution calling on George Brown to stay on as leader.

Party leadership was decided at entirely different gatherings. The élite would get together over dinner and drinks at a private club or perhaps at someone's home, and there, from among the people present, a party leader was chosen.

Confederation did not bring any immediate change to the established pattern, except that the party élite found themselves sitting as members of Parliament.

The British practices were firmly entrenched in the processes of the new Canadian Parliament. The practice by which a political party leader was chosen through a confidential sounding of the party's sitting MPs became the norm here, as it was in Britain. If a party was in power, the man chosen to be leader by the party's élite had to be approved by the governor general, as this person would become the new prime minister. In many cases, the government party simple deferred to the governor general's wishes in choosing their leader; however, it was expected that the governor general would conduct a sounding of the party's MPs to arrive at his choice. It was a very civilized procedure. The governor general would consult the retiring leader and other key parliamentarians on their choice for party leader. In effect, the retiring prime minister would often anoint his successor.

John A. Macdonald was the first party leader to be selected or confirmed in his position by the governor general. Macdonald's Tories had won a decisive victory in the 1867 election, and the party's élite was behind the choice of Macdonald as the country's first prime minister and official leader of the party in the House. Lord Monck, then the Governor General, told Macdonald informally that he would be called upon to lead the Tory government. However, the deciding factor in Macdonald's nomination as prime minister was not his leadership role in the Conservative party but rather a combination of his role in the negotiations that led to Confederation and his work in the pre-Confederation provincial government. Factors such as the size of the Tory majority and the fact that Macdonald's caucus rallied behind him were secondary to Monck.

The royal prerogative, as represented by the governor general, was even more evident in the five years following Macdonald's death in 1891. The Conservative party was split into various factions, all of which were vying for control.

Hector Langevin, whom many saw as Macdonald's heir apparent, was embroiled in a controversy surrounding his management of the Department of Public Works. Two other possible successors to Macdonald turned down the leadership of the Tories. Sir Charles Tupper was then the Canadian high commissioner in London and claimed to have no interest in the position, while John Thompson, a long-time parliamentarian, refused the position on the grounds that as a Roman Catholic, he could not unite the largely Protestant caucus behind him. In desperation, the governor general asked Thompson to suggest a suitable leader for the Tories. Thompson was thus granted a major role and responsibility in shaping Canada's government following Macdonald's death. Thompson suggested J. J. C. Abbott for the leadership. Abbott was, at the time, the only member of caucus who did not belong to one of the factions. He could exercise a caretaker role until the party was once again united and another leader could be selected. Abbott accepted the governor general's invitation to form the next government.

Almost a year later, Abbott resigned. In his letter of resignation to the governor general, Abbott suggested that Thompson be named to succeed him, thereby returning an earlier favour. During Abbott's year and a half at the helm, the party had worked out many of its divisions, especially the religious ones, so Thompson's leadership had become possible. However, Thompson's sudden death in 1894 once again left the party and the country without a leader. Although the majority of the Conservative caucus wanted Sir Charles Tupper to be named prime minister, Governor General Aberdeen and his wife refused to accept him. Aberdeen, unable to come up with a suitable replacement, wrote to the colonial secretary in London for help. The colonial secretary wrote back that in his opinion, Mackenzie Bowell, who was then acting prime minister and Tory leader, should be asked to form the government. The colonial secretary's advice was followed. We see that although Canada was nominally an independent country, the choice of its leader was imposed from London over the heads of the party's caucus.

Bowell's grasp on power was tenuous at best. He did not have the party's backing, and in addition, he sat in the Senate, from which he couldn't face the opposition or control his own caucus in the House of Commons. Finally, in early 1896, just months before an election call was due, seven members of the cabinet resigned. Bowell, faced with an open rebellion against his leadership, twice offered to resign, but both times Aberdeen refused to accept his resignation. Trying to prevent Tupper from taking over as leader and prime minister had become an obsession. The governor general did not believe Tupper had the proper leadership qualities. It also appears that Aberdeen's wife had a profound personal dislike for Tupper.

This governmental and constitutional crisis was ended with an agreement that allowed Tupper to lead the government in the House while Bowell continued as prime minister. The agreement further stipulated that Bowell would step down when the term ended, although Aberdeen was noncommittal on whether he would allow Tupper to become prime minister. Still, 1896 was a turning point in Canadian politics because it was the year when a political party asserted its right to select its own leader independent of the wishes of the governor general. From this point on, the governor general's role was reduced to rubber-stamping the caucus decision in leadership selection.

For the parties in opposition, selecting a leader was no less problematic, even if the choice did not require vice-regal approval. In 1867, the opposition benches were filled by a disparate group of members representing a number of parties with little or no organization. The opposition had no leader and didn't seem inclined to select one. Although British tradition called for the naming of a leader for the opposition, usually the leader of the party with the second-largest number of MPs in the House, Brown and his reformers did not seem inclined to honour tradition by taking over the official opposition's role. The government party was forced to step in to select a leader for the opposition. Sandfield MacDonald, a Reform Party MP, was chosen by the Tories to be leader of the opposition. MacDonald notwithstanding, it was Alexander Mackenzie who emerged as the main opposition spokesperson between 1867 and 1872. The near-defeat of the Conservatives in 1872 and the respectable showing of his Liberals convinced Mackenzie that the opposition Liberals should select an official leader around whom they could rally in the House and on the electoral hustings.

A committee made up of the Liberal Party's leadership, both inside and outside the House, was struck to select the party's opposition leader, and Mackenzie was its overwhelming choice. When the Liberals gained power in 1874, the governor general promptly named Mackenzie prime minister. Following the Liberals' defeat two years later, Mackenzie wrote to his caucus to resign and asked them to select a new leader for the opposition. The caucus rejected Mackenzie's resignation, and he stayed on as leader until 1880. During this period, the Liberal parliamentary group grew increasingly uneasy with Mackenzie's leadership, and eventually five members of his caucus, led by Edward Blake, confronted Mackenzie to ask him to step down. Within two years, Mackenzie had gone from reluctant draftee for a position from which he wanted to resign to unwelcome hanger-on. Mackenzie resigned on April 28, 1880. The Liberal caucus met shortly thereafter to elect a new leader.

Consistent with British traditions, the meeting to elect a new Liberal leader was restricted to the party's MPs. Edward Blake, the leader of the revolt against Mackenzie, was unanimously selected by the caucus to replace him. Blake subsequently led the party to two election defeats before he resigned for health reasons. Blake's successor, Wilfrid Laurier, was, like his predecessor, chosen at a closed-door meeting of the caucus.

Laurier began two Canadian leadership traditions. He was the first Liberal leader to be chosen by his predecessor, a tradition that remained until Pierre Trudeau's resignation. The second tradition stemmed from Laurier's interest in the American political process, for it was under Laurier's tenure as Liberal leader that the first party convention was held in Canada.

Although many other names were being mentioned as replacements for Blake, Laurier emerged as Blake's handpicked successor, a choice the party caucus officially confirmed on June 7, 1887, and Laurier accepted on June 23.

The Conservatives selected only one leader while in opposition between 1850 and 1920. Following the Conservative defeat in 1990, Tupper resigned as party leader. George Foster, the heir apparent to Tupper, had also lost his seat in the election debacle; although this loss did not disqualify him for the leadership, it was a significant handicap in the eyes of the parliamentary caucus. Sir Charles Tupper's son was considered by some to be the next-best choice for leader, but he was ultimately rejected, the caucus fearing charges of Tory nepotism. The caucus met twice in early months of 1901 to choose a successor to Tupper. Robert Borden's name emerged from the discussions of the first meeting and, although he originally declined the leader's post, he was persuaded to reconsider at the caucus's second meeting.

When Borden announced his resignation in 1919, the governor general asked him who should be considered to succeed him. Borden was unsure, although he appears to have favoured Sir Thomas White, who had been minister of Finance from 1911 to 1917. To arrive at his recommendation, Borden asked all the members of the Tory caucus to provide him with their choices for leader, in writing. They were to rank their choices, if they had more than one. The results of the ballots, as Borden called them, showed that Arthur Meighen was the overwhelming choice of the back-benchers while White came out as the choice of the cabinet. However, when second and third choices were considered, Meighen was the overall favourite. Despite these results, Borden recommended to the governor general that White be asked to form the next government. Borden's reasoning was that the leader would have to work with the cabinet and that it was thus better to follow the recommendation of the cabinet than that of the back benches. When White declined the governor general's offer, Borden suggested Meighen as the next-best choice, after convincing his cabinet to accept Meighen as leader. That was the first time that such an exhaustive consultation was undertaken, but Borden's ballots simply replaced the closed-door meetings; no sounding of the extra-parliamentary wing occurred. That would come with the introduction of the political convention into Canadian political life.

LEADERSHIP SELECTION, 1920 TO THE PRESENT

The Liberal Party was the first to select a leader through a national leadership convention. That first leadership convention was largely a product of circumstance; however, the idea for a national party convention had been around for some time. The idea originated with Laurier and J. J. Willison, the editor of the *Globe* newspaper. That such a meeting would eventually choose Laurier's successor was unforeseen.

The Liberal Party had first held a policy convention in 1893, as a means of raising the party's morale and preparing for an election. The Conservative government at the time was floundering, and Laurier felt that a unified Liberal Party could be victorious in the next election.

Willison, a close friend of Laurier's, had written a number of articles on the 1892 American Democratic Party convention and was convinced that a similar type of meeting was just what the Liberals needed to put some wind in their sails. Willison proposed to Laurier that the Liberals hold a convention, gathering delegates from across the country. Although

American conventions were primarily held to nominate a presidential candidate, they also served as a forum at which the electoral platforms of the parties were established. Therefore, Willison argued in a letter to Laurier, a similar convention could be held where the Liberal election platform could be ratified. Such a meeting could also serve as an occasion to show that the party was fully behind Laurier's leadership. Laurier agreed to Willison's plan as he, too, had long been an admirer of the American political system, and especially of its conventions. Laurier modified the American model to fit his particular aims, and a convention was called for 1893. The convention was originally conceived as a "policy conference," composed of delegates from across the country. While the U.S. model was strictly a leadership convention, Laurier would use the concept as the means to set down the party's policies following the war. At that time, the convention further provided a forum for airing the party's unity problems, which were a consequence of the conscription crisis. The meeting proved a resounding success, and Laurier claimed it as a deciding factor in the Liberal victory in the subsequent election.

Considering the success of the 1893 convention, it is not surprising that Laurier later proposed to resort to the same forum, the convention in 1919, to reunite a Liberal Party badly divided by the issue of conscription. Borden had capitalized on this issue to maintain his unionist coalition in government, the Liberal and Tory MPs who favoured conscription, at the same time causing a major rift in Canadian society. Conscriptionist English Canada rallied against Québécois society, which opposed such a measure. This French-English split was evident in the House of Commons, where the English Liberal MPs chose to leave their party to sit on the government benches as part of Borden's coalition. With the war behind them, Laurier proposed to hold a convention that would provide an opportunity for the Liberal members of the unionist government to return to the Liberal party. Originally the convention was scheduled for late 1919 or early 1920 and would have been similar in format to the Liberal convention of 1893. However, Laurier's death in February 1919 altered the convention's purpose.

Traditionally, Laurier's successor should have emerged from a closed-door meeting of the caucus. However, as a result of the election of 1917, the Liberal Party had a predominately French-Catholic composition; more than three-quarters of its members represented Québec ridings. Much of the anglophone Protestant wing of the Liberal Party had joined Borden's government. Any leader who emerged from the caucus would probably have represented this French-Catholic majority. Such a choice would have been the kiss of death to the Liberals' election chances. To reunite the party and renew it with an electoral victory, the party had to be led by an anglophone. W. S. Fielding, one of Laurier's former cabinet colleagues, was put forward as a successor, but the party's Québec deputies refused to accept Fielding. The Québec MPs were angry over Fielding's desertion of Laurier in the thick of the conscription debate. Three others were considered as possible successors to Laurier — Mackenzie King, G. P. Graham, and W. M. Martin. None of these men had a seat in Parliament, however, and tradition made holding a parliamentary seat a condition of leadership. Unable to resolve the leadership question among themselves, the caucus finally decided that the whole issue had to be decided by the upcoming convention.

The official announcement by the caucus gave no special attention to the leadership question. The meeting was held August 5–7, 1919, and the agenda included the party electoral platform, organization, and, as if as an afterthought, the leadership question.

For most Liberal insiders, the selection of a new leader through a convention was a measure forced upon the party by the linguistic and religious divisions in the caucus. It was not to be expected that the next leader of the Liberal Party would be similarly selected. Even Mackenzie King, who was the party's choice at this first leadership convention, was of the opinion that the next leader should be once again chosen by his caucus.

If the convention was a new phenomenon at the federal level, such gatherings had been held to select leaders at the provincial level before 1919. In Ontario, the provincial Liberals chose their leader through a convention just weeks before the federal Liberals did so. These conventions were relatively popular in the Western provinces, probably as a result of the influence of the American political model in the West.

As in the American model, the winner of the Liberal Party's convention was to be elected by at least 50 per cent of the votes cast by the delegates present. The balloting would be secret, unlike the U.S. practice of using a roll-call vote. Every delegate at the convention was issued a booklet of ballots, numbered one to ten. Delegates were instructed to use the ballot corresponding to the round of voting.

Although many leaders of the party favoured a roll-call, the organizing committee decided against it on grounds that such an open display might undermine the fragile unity of the party at a time when the language and religious divisions were so close to the surface. Most people, for example, expected the Québec delegation to vote as a bloc against Fielding. As Fielding seemed favoured in other provinces, a roll-call vote might have been dangerous to the party's unity. Thereafter, the secret ballot was retained and has since become the fixture of our leadership-selection process.

The delegates for the convention were chosen at delegate-selection meetings, which had to be held at least one month before the convention. Each riding elected three delegates, based on simple majority votes. The remaining delegates, as is still the case today, were party officials from the federal or provincial wings of the party. For the first time in Canadian history, the input of a party's extraparliamentary wing was sought in selecting its leader. The Liberal convention was a successful experiment, and in 1927, the Tories followed the Liberal lead as they, too, chose their leader through a national convention.

The genesis for the Conservative leadership convention of 1927 was an open revolt against the leadership of Arthur Meighen, who had been chosen leader in 1920 through Borden's informal ballot of his caucus. Several prominent Tories from Montréal and Winnipeg were dissatisfied with Meighen, and despite the fact that his leadership had been reconfirmed in 1921, they launched a frontal attack against him.

Meighen held on, and no mechanism existed to replace him, unless he chose to resign. The dissidents were not deterred. Unable to change the leader under existing rules, they decided to change the way the leader was chosen. In 1923, committees were organized in Québec and Manitoba to push for a leadership convention to choose Meighen's successor. That same year, the Ontario wing of the Tories endorsed a motion supporting such a change. Later that year, at a meeting attended by Meighen and the party's parliamentary caucus, a similar proposal for reform was voted on and passed. Obviously the Liberal Party had opened a Pandora's box. It would never again be possible to choose a political party leader through the traditional method of the caucus meeting. The extraparliamentary caucus would henceforth demand inclusion in this all-important decision.

Meighen resigned in 1926, following another smashing election defeat, in which he had lost his own seat. Even if

Meighen had chosen his successor, the reform movement had gained sufficient support to get the caucus to reject his authority. As the Liberals had done, the Conservatives hoped that holding a convention might help the party to rebuild following their two crushing electoral defeats.

Six candidates ran for the leadership of the Tories in 1927, and in the end, R. B. Bennett was chosen over Hugh Guthrie. Bennett had received only six votes more than he required to win. The Tories' experience with the leadership convention proved positive when they were returned to power in 1930.

The national convention may have begun with a Liberal desire to follow the American example of representative democracy in selecting a leaders, but it was established as an institution through association with electoral victory. By copying the Liberal experiment, the Conservatives hoped that a "one-time only" leadership convention would quell the dissent at the grass-roots level and reunite the party, from which point the normal processes and institutions of the party would continue as before. That the convention outlived its original temporary purpose is a good indication that once the people were involved in the leadership-selection process, they were not inclined to return to the decision-making sidelines.

The CCF/NDP Leadership Selection

The Co-operative Commonwealth Federation (CCF), founded in 1932, and its successor, the New Democratic Party (NDP), founded in 1961, have roots that go back to the progressive social-reform movements of the 1920s and 1930s. In the first few years following the formation of the CCF, it continued to function largely as a social movement, reflecting its origins. It had no designated leader, nor did it have a single spokesperson to convey its message. By the time the CCF organized as a political party, the leadership convention was the means by which the two major political parties selected their leaders. It was natural for the newly formed party to elect its first leader in the same way.

The leader of the CCF was elected in 1932 at the first policy convention of the party in Calgary. J. S. Woodsworth was unanimously elected as the party's president, a title given to denote the leader's responsibility over both the parliamentary and the extraparliamentary wings of the party. Woodsworth had a distinguished career prior to his involvement with the CCF. First elected to the Commons in 1921, he had become, over the years, the unofficial leader of a group of disgruntled United Farmer and Progressive MPs, which had come to be known as the "ginger group." Woodsworth had inherited the CCF's presidency for the simple reason that no other person of his political stature or experience represented the party in the House at the time, although Woodsworth would soon be joined by a number of talented and committed CCF MPs. With Woodsworth as its leader, the CCF received instant credibility in the House, although some MPs from the two established parties were loath to admit it.

From its beginnings, the CCF established a tradition of biannual leadership reviews, a tradition that the NDP has continued. At every meeting of the national CCF, a leader's position could be challenged, though in practice all CCF/NDP leaders have retired on their own terms and not as a consequence of the review process.

When Woodsworth resigned, the 1940 convention had just been held. The leader's post was left vacant until the next scheduled meeting of the party, in 1942. An interim leader was chosen by the caucus to lead the party in the House until then. M. J. Coldwell, the CCF's first national secretary and national chairperson, was named interim leader. The unhurried leadership selection process stems directly from the CCF's roots as a social movement in which an individual's leadership was considered less important than the actions of the collective membership. The 1942 Toronto convention chose Coldwell to replace Woodsworth, and he, like Woodsworth, was elected without opposition.

By the time of Coldwell's resignation in 1958, the CCF was becoming an increasingly marginal party with little electoral support. Negotiations had been going on for a number of years with the Canadian labour movement to create a new political party. These negotiations seemed close to fruition, meaning that Coldwell's successor would most likely be the last leader of the CCF, although it was likely that this person would eventually inherit the leadership of the new party.

The last leader of the CCF was Hazen Argue, a man of almost boundless ambition. Argue was elected House leader by the caucus in 1958 by a one-vote margin. At the Regina convention of the CCF in 1960, Argue was, again, the only candidate for the party's presidency. However, the party was split over the issue of his leadership. He had the complete support of the CCF's parliamentary wing, but was unpopular with the extraparliamentary élite of the party. In the end, a compromise was reached that confirmed the entrenched power of the extraparliamentary élite of the CCF. Argue was to be named national leader, but the presidency of the party would be left vacant until the party's next convention. There would be, of course, no other CCF convention, as plans were already being made for the founding convention of the new party for the following year.

The founding convention of the NDP in 1961 was to be the occasion for a showdown between Hazen Argue and T. C. Douglas. The rift between the caucus and the extraparliamentary élite of the party had not been resolved, and Douglas was drafted to run against Argue. Douglas was, at the time, the only CCF provincial premier, and he was an extremely effective speaker whom many saw as the man who could lead the new party to electoral success. In addition, many of the party hierarchy supported Douglas because they feared that Argue would deliver the nascent NDP into the hands of the Liberals if he were elected leader. The 1961 Ottawa convention turned out to be no contest, as Douglas beat Argue on the first ballot by more than a thousand votes. The size of Douglas's margin of victory emphasized the strength of the organized-labour support that backed Douglas. A disgruntled Argue eventually crossed the Commons floor to join the Liberals before being named to a Senate seat. As for Douglas, he was to lead the party in its formative years before retiring for health and personal reasons in 1971.

Democracy and Representation

The development of the leadership-selection process for the three main political parties seemed a major step forward in democratization. Not so. The process of leadership selection soon became corrupted and manipulated by party élites. From the outset, the delegates to conventions usually represented the local élites rather than their ridings' population. Meetings were often held with little prior notice. Votes were bought and meetings packed to elect one delegate over another. The abuses we have seen during recent leadership contests go back to the very foundation of the system.

Money has been an issue since the first conventions. From the outset, leadership candidates tried to outspend their rivals on the assumption that doing so was the key to victory. While today's funds are spent on advertising or polling, the spending in yesteryear went towards lavish entertainment for influential party members. In the early leadership contests, the moneyed élites wielded considerable influence over the final decisions of the convention. Although our leadership conventions were never decided by the backroom boys to the extent that American conventions have been, we have come close. Even the best-intentioned parties have adopted features that have undermined the democratic ideals behind their leadership-selection processes. With the Liberals and Conservatives, the main source of discrepancy is the undue weight of the non-elected *ex officio* delegate group at their conventions. These representatives of the party hierarchy can swing a convention away from a popularly supported candidate to a less popular candidate who is riding the party machine. In the NDP conventions, the delegate positions granted to trade unions have the same effect. Union backing enabled David Lewis to beat James Laxer in 1970, and Ed Broadbent to beat Rosemary Brown in 1975.

Although the present process is, in theory, a more democratic one than the closed-door, caucus-type leadership-selection process that we inherited from England, it has not really lived up to democratic ideals. There have been abuses by all parties, and the whole system is in need of a major overhaul.

5

LOOKING SOUTH AND ABROAD

As Canadians, we are admirably proud of our political system, but this pride sometimes leads us to be critical of and patronizing towards U.S. political institutions. Yet the U.S. system reflects a serious belief in the words "government of the people, for the people, by the people." By the time the Republicans and Democrats choose their presidential candidates, each nominee has received millions of votes in the course of the primaries.

Casual observers of the American political scene, and its critics, will argue that the American system of presidential nomination is set up to test candidates in the spotlight of competition through a number of caucuses and primaries that lead to national office. The philosophy that underlies the process is that the rights of the individual are supremely important. Thus, the rules of selecting candidates for political office in the United States are entrenched in state and national legislation, ensuring that the rights of the people are not usurped by the political parties or the state. That was not always the case.

In the early years of the Republic, the American political process drew on British political tradition. In time, more indigenous forms of political participation developed. One of the first was the caucus.

The caucus is the oldest form of nominating system; its roots go back to the period just prior to the War of Independence. At the outset, the caucus gathered the town notables, who decided who was to occupy the various local offices. With the development of party politics following independence, each party would hold its meeting to decide its candidates. Elections, open only to the merchants and landowners, subsequently decided the outcome. Eventually, the widening of the franchise enabled all persons to vote for the candidate of their choice, although the nominating system, with its closed-door meeting of the party élites, continued to decide who these candidates were to be.

As more elected offices were created at the local, state, and national levels, the caucuses were gradually opened up to include all interested party members.

The modern caucus for presidential nomination is a multi-level process beginning with local or district caucuses and culminating in a state-wide caucus, where the delegates for the national party conventions are chosen. In fact, by the time the state-wide caucus is held, the results obtained by the local caucuses may be completely altered.

By the 1900s, state governments began to legislate the nominating process, thus wrenching control from the parties. The states first undertook to supervise the caucuses and, in time, took over their organization. Although parties at first resisted this involvement by the states, it proved popular with the electorate, and they soon relented. The party élites were moved out in favour of democracy.

Besides caucuses, American candidates for political office are also selected through a primary election. Primaries can best be described as caucuses with a ballot-box. A primary is, in all but name, an election. Primaries are a creation of the state governments in their effort to hand over to the people the prerogative of candidate selection. In 1988, twenty-seven states (the largest number to date) held primaries, during which the voters got to voice their preference for presidential candidates. There are many variations to this process. In some cases, delegates are apportioned according to the percentage of votes received by the presidential candidate; these delegates are appointed by the candidate's organization. In other cases, persons wishing to become delegates state which candidate they support, and they are elected based on this notice. Finally, in some cases, the candidate who wins a primary wins all the delegates. There is no federal direction to encourage the adoption of primaries and no federal regulations except those covering election financing, matching funds, and the electoral process. There is a movement to create a federally legislated national primary. As with the caucuses, the sole aim of a primary is to select delegates who will represent constituents at the national conventions. Once again, the states have increasingly made their presence felt in this final stage of the presidential nomination process by increasingly forcing, by law, delegates to vote exactly as instructed by their constituents. As national party conventions rely on a non-secret vote, these laws have proved highly effective.

Thus, through the caucus and primary process, the American people get a direct say who their presidential candidates will be. It needs to be noted that the presidency is not the only post for which candidates are selected by primary or caucus. In fact, the American political process has remained close to its post-independence roots, as all political offices in the United States are contested within the parties through primaries or caucuses before the actual election day.

The primary/caucus process culminates with national conventions where the presidential candidate for each party is elected. This nominee stands as flag-bearer for the party and its political agenda, which he or she may have helped to mould, but not as party leader, as in the case in Canadian political parties. The actual party leadership in an American party rests in the hands of the congressional leader or the party chairperson. However, many of the developments that helped to democratize the American process do not date back to the revolution, but rather find their source of inspiration in the McGovern–Fraser report of 1968.

Until the 1968 Democratic convention, conventions and delegate-selection meetings were controlled by a select group of back-room boys. That convention nominated Hubert Humphrey, a choice forced upon the convention by the party élites. Amid controversy concerning the fairness, representativeness, and legitimacy of the nomination process as it existed then, the Democratic party formed a commission to look into the process of presidential nomination and suggest reforms. The McGovern–Fraser Commission, as it came to be known, tabled its report at the end of 1968. It concluded that the nominating process, from the local to the national level, was in need of major reform if it was to live up to the democratic ideals that it was supposed to embody. Among the commission's recommendations was the elimination of certain types of primary contests favouring the party organization, such as "winner-take-all primaries," where the winning candidate could gain all of a state's delegates without winning a majority of the vote. More important, the recommendations addressed the issue of representation, a problem that had plagued the national convention process since its inception. Conventions were characteristically dominated by white males. To correct this situation, the formation of party associations for women and minorities was encouraged.

The Commission's report provoked debate about the state of the nominating process. As a consequence of this debate, a number of important changes were suggested to make delegate selection more democratic. The commission's recommendations were well received. State legislatures controlled by Democrats redrafted and altered their primary and caucus legislation. Republican-controlled legislatures also acted at the behest of the Democrats to implement the required changes in the laws that governed Democratic primaries. However, in many instances, the Republican party's own primaries were reformed along similar lines by the state legislatures, a move that the national-level Republicans protested against but could not prevent.

What most of us see of a national convention is the television coverage of the balloons and streamers, the delegates gathered under the banners of their respective states, the voting, the victory speech, and the call to party unity. I went to the 1952 Republican convention in Chicago and was overwhelmed by the splendour of the event. Images stay with me still: Tom Dewey, the party's presidential standard-bearer in 1948, waiting in line for coffee and sandwiches; the flowing oratory of Senator Everett Dirksen of Illinois, highlighting the traditional cleavage in the party between the hard-line conservatives and the Eastern Seaboard moderates; the grand entrance of Gen. Douglas MacArthur and his "old soldiers never die" military oration before the delegates; the non-stop buttonholing and talking of Clare Booth Luce; John Foster Dulles cloaked in neutrality in his box at the edge of the convention floor; and, finally, Dwight Eisenhower and the young Senator Richard Nixon, together with their wives, accepting the victory plaudits of the delegates at the end of the convention. These were the images, but the important elements of the political manoeuvring were not visible on the floor.

Most of the North American public assumed that Eisenhower would ride to an easy victory. In fact, the Taft forces were initially in control. Robert Taft had a formidable record in the U.S. Senate and was chairman of the Republican National Committee.

I had turned to a friend, Governor Bob Bradford of Massachusetts, with a request for his help to get me into the convention as an interested spectator. He couldn't arrange that, he told me, because Senator Taft was RNC chairman (in Canadian terms, he was the party leader and president), and his position gave him absolute control over the party and its machinery, including entrance privileges to the convention. Bradford was a known Eisenhower sympathizer, and he held out no hope that his recommendation would get me a ticket. I persisted in my determination to go and finally was sworn in as an honorary assistant sergeant-at-arms for the Massachusetts delegation. Later, the national television audience would hear the convention chairman repeatedly calling out, as he pounded his gavel, "Sergeants-at-arms, clear the aisles." If the viewers had visions of burly officers clearing the aisles of delegates, they were wrong; so many sergeants-at-arms had been sworn in as a means to by-pass the convention restrictions that we jammed all the aisles and corners in the hall.

A controversy among the Southern delegates involved those from Florida, Georgia, Kansas, Mississippi, Missouri, and Texas — the latter two states being the most important because of the numbers of delegates involved. For each of these states, two delegations showed up at the convention, one delegation that overwhelmingly supported Senator Taft and another that was leaning towards Eisenhower. This situation occurred largely because of Eisenhower's success in drawing in a large number of Independent, Democrat, and disenchanted Republican voters. In the primaries and caucuses, these "new" voters tended to support delegates favourable to the Eisenhower candidacy, but by no overwhelming margin. The Taft forces saw in this grass-roots movement a potential threat to Taft's candidacy and, working through the state parties, challenged the delegates' credentials, the process by which they were selected, and Eisenhower's integrity.

The state parties began removing the convention delegates who had been selected and replacing them with "regular" delegates of their choice. By doing so, the State Party Committee voided the caucus and primary results in the Southern states. The voters' choice was being ignored. In one case, Georgia, the State Party went to the state's supreme court to have the results of the primary declared void. The court agreed and authorized the party to choose its own delegates for the convention. Eisenhower vowed a fight.

Thus, when the delegates convened in Chicago on July 1, the two factions for each state showed up — the "regular" delegation, which had been appointed by the party and supported Taft, and the "illegals," whose credentials had been voided and who tended to support Eisenhower. The Eisenhower forces planned to challenge the right of the appointed delegates to be recognized by the convention. For his part, Taft had arranged to take the issue to the Republican National Committee's Credentials Committee. This body had the final word on all questions related to the choice and seating of delegates. By doing so, Taft hoped to have his delegates from the South recognized by an official body that would quell the debate. The National Committee was overwhelmingly weighted with Taft supporters. In every case taken to the Credentials Committee relating to the disputed state delegations, Taft delegations were endorsed by a 3-to-2 vote margin. These decisions meant that Taft now had an overwhelming lead in a pre-convention delegate count. (As a result of the Credentials Committee's decisions, the Taft forces could count on 530 votes, and Eisenhower on 427, with 604 needed to nominate.)

On the first official day of the convention, the Eisenhower forces struck a decisive blow to the Taft forces and their manipulation of the delegate-selection process. Eisenhower, who had vowed to fight back, pressured the convention into addressing the issue. Claiming that the wishes of the voters weren't being respected, the Eisenhower delegation, led by Henry Cabot Lodge, moved to have the convention decide which Southern delegation would be permitted to sit at the convention. At this point, the main states at issue were Louisiana, Texas, and Georgia. Conventions traditionally opened with a consideration of amendments and changes to the party rules, and Lodge managed to get the delegate-seating issue considered at that time.

The opening session looked at an amendment to the party's rules that would permit the whole convention to vote on the issue of which Southern delegation would be allowed to sit. The results of the vote were 658 to 548 in favour of having the delegate-seating issue considered by the whole convention. This vote was widely interpreted as a victory for the Eisenhower over the Taft forces, and it provided Eisenhower with the momentum that eventually carried him to the nomination. In addition, on another vote to exclude the contested delegates from voting on the issue of delegate seating, the Taft forces capitulated in the face of the convention's support for a review of the situation, and the motion to exclude the contested delegations from voting was unanimously endorsed.

On July 10, the convention looked at the delegate-seating issue directly. Delegations from Texas and Georgia were up for consideration. The Eisenhower troops demanded a formal roll-call vote, as they feared that the convention chairperson, a Taft supporter, might decide in favour of the Taft forces if a simple voice vote were taken. The vote would deal with each state separately, with Georgia first. Thus, on the issue of recognizing the delegations that had originally been selected by primary over the "regulars" appointed by the party, the

Eisenhower forces won 607 votes to 531 in favour of the former. The results stunned the Taft forces, and they were obliged to withdraw their support for the "regular" Texas delegation. The Texas issue wasn't brought to a vote. The Taft forces had conceded defeat in the face of grass-roots party. As a result of these reversals of the Credentials Committee's decisions, the unofficial delegate count favoured Eisenhower 501 to 485.

On July 11, General Eisenhower won the Republican nomination for president by 845 to 280 in the revised first-ballot tally (the original count was 595 for Eisenhower and 500 for Taft). Clearly Eisenhower's victory on the delegate-seating issue was a tactical and moral victory over the Taft candidacy.

What this story highlights are the pitfalls of letting a party have sole control over its nomination process. In this particular case, the party leadership contravened state laws and its own rules to stack the delegate count in favour of its own candidate, Senator Taft, who happened to be National Committee chairman, over an "outsider." Since this incident, numerous changes have been made at both the state and the party levels to prevent similar abuses of power. State laws now more precisely define who can vote in a primary, as well as who can run for a delegate position. Depending on the state in which the primary is run, any registered voter can participate. In some states, one may vote only in the primary of the party for which one is registered, and in others one may vote in the primary of choice, or in both — or more, depending on the number of parties involved. Taft's main argument was that the Eisenhower forces had used illegal means in their recruitment of Independents and Democrats to vote in the primaries; it turns out that Eisenhower's efforts did comply with state laws of the time. Furthermore, there are now more primaries and fewer caucuses to select presidential nominees or delegates for the conventions. In 1952, most delegates were chosen in caucuses or state conventions. The latter tended to favour "at large" delegates over those that had come up from the precinct-level primaries. Finally, the parties themselves have cleaned up their operations as a result of the McGovern–Fraser Commission report.

What about the Canadian case? The kind of manipulation Taft was capable of is possible, even probable, in Canada. The recent Progressive Conservative leadership convention and both the Liberals' leadership and leadership-review conventions were marked by similar irregularities in their delegate-selection process. In the case of the NDP, the support of the union leadership is a prerequisite for party leadership. If the parties can't police themselves, who will? It's obvious Canada is due for its own McGovern–Fraser report.

The campaign to become president of the United States commences well in advance of the opening of the primary races. Numerous analysts have pointed out that the U.S. system is geared towards a perpetual race for the presidency. A good illustration of this permanent candidacy and how American law makes it possible is the case of Ronald Reagan. Reagan's campaign began long before he officially announced his intention to run.

Ronald Reagan dedicated his post-acting career to the pursuit of political office — first in California, where he was elected governor, then nationally. His interest in elective office began while he was president of the Screen Actors Guild, and he subsequently became an avowed member of the conservative wing of the Republican Party.

Reagan's political star began to rise in 1964 when he was asked by conservative Republican candidate for president Barry Goldwater to read a speech on television in support of the Goldwater candidacy. That appearance attracted the attention of a number of prominent conservative business people who did not fail to realize Reagan's political potential. Among these men were William French Smith, who subsequently served as Reagan's attorney general, and Justin Dunt, the president of Kraft Foods. These men, and others, became Reagan's political advisers and financial backers.

Beginning in 1966, they invested, on Reagan's behalf, large sums of money to free him from financial worry and enable him to devote himself full-time to the quest for the governor's chair. Reagan won the governorship and began to implement the conservative agenda his backers had pushed.

In 1975, Reagan's backers urged him to enter a new race, that for president of the United States. To Reagan's backers, Gerry Ford was not conservative enough in his policies. Reagan's team raised the necessary funds to enter the race, but Reagan subsequently bowed out for strategic reasons. Noting the inevitability of Carter's victory, the Reagan team saw more political points in Reagan's support of the Ford ticket than in a second-place finish. Furthermore, Reagan's conservative agenda was not well received by the voters during the primaries. Bowing out of the race would give the Reagan team a chance to better tailor their policies to the American electorate. Reagan thus chose to bide his time and consolidate his position for the race in 1980.

Reagan left the 1976 race with $1 million unspent, with which his team set up a Political Action Committee (PAC), under his control. A PAC is an organization registered with the federal government. Its sole purpose is to promote a particular political agenda. PACs are permitted by law to raise funds and spend them in pursuit of this agenda. Although they are prohibited from directly financing particular candidates for office, they are permitted to disburse funds to promote individual candidacies.

PACs use their fund-raising apparatus to boost funding for a particular campaign in two ways. First, the PAC may share its lists of contributors and its mailing and phone lists with campaign organizations. Second, it may itself contact its contributors, asking them for financial support for a particular candidate's campaign.

Reagan's PAC allowed him to hire a full-time staff and to guarantee himself a limited income as its administrator. In fact, Reagan's second run for the presidency began months after the Republican convention had confirmed Ford's candidacy.

The PAC also allowed Reagan to establish some important political IOUs, which he subsequently cashed in during his second run for the presidency. Reagan used money from the PAC to aid the campaigns of nearly 250 conservative candidates for a variety of local, state, and national offices. By the time of his second run for the nomination, Reagan was able to count on the support of a large number of conservatives he had himself supported between 1976 and 1980. Reagan also financed his unofficial campaign through a syndicated television commentary and newspaper column, as well as numerous speaking engagements arranged by Speaking Bureau, Inc., his own company. In all, his combined earnings from these activities were approximately $500,000 for about eight months' work. Once Reagan entered the primary race in 1979, Speaking Bureau, Inc., and his PAC dissolved, and their staff were subsequently rehired by the Reagan campaign for the presidency!

Some critics now argue that the American system, with its divergent state laws, has become a maze with lawyers guiding candidates through the nomination process, thus diluting the direct democracy Americans are so proud to espouse. Recent nominating conventions for both parties have shown remarkably little surprise at their outcome. Early in the primaries and caucuses, the financial strains lead candidates to drop out of the race. Others, because of the futility of the cause, choose to withdraw early and try again next time, as

Reagan did in 1976. For most, except the best organized and financed, the almost six months of primaries prove an unmanageable burden. Despite the ideals and the process, the eventual winner emerges early in the race and has never, in recent years, been upset. Reagan is perhaps the best modern example of the front-runner advantage. To equalize the chances, some have moved the idea of a one-time, nationally or regionally controlled primary, organized by the federal government. The financial component of the nominating process would thereby be minimized and the process would be much more broadly based than is currently the case. In addition, such a national primary would finally give all Americans a chance to choose from a full slate of candidates. At present, as candidates leave the race for various reasons, those unfortunate enough to live in states with late primaries get to choose only among the three or so that have managed to tough it out. A national or regional primary would give all voters in all states an equal say in their choice for party leader.

BRITAIN AND FRANCE

Of course, Canada's political institutions also draw on their European heritage, especially from Britain, which has served as the model for many modern democracies. If we look strictly at the choice of party leader, the United States has widened the franchise considerably compared to France or Britain. In both of these countries, the choice of party leader remains the prerogative of the party élites, very much like the U.S. pre-independence model or, closer to home, Canada's own method for leadership selection before the advent of the conventions.

Until the 1970s, the British Conservative and Labour parties selected their leaders through a similar method. A caucus of the parliamentary wing of the party would meet in secret to choose a new leader from among its sitting MPs. The extra-parliamentary wing of the parties was excluded from the decision. When a party occupied the government benches, the new leader would also become the prime minister.

The traditional leadership-selection process changed little over the years. However, in 1974, an open challenge to then prime minister Edward Heath led to the first open caucus. The eventual winner of this first-ever open caucus was Margaret Thatcher. Her successor, John Major, was selected by the same method.

Here's how that open caucus works. Under the rules that existed in 1974, the Tories had no defined procedure for calling for leadership review. The party leader held the post until he or she resigned or died. Heath wasn't interested in stepping down, but he was increasingly unable to steer his heavily divided party in Parliament. He turned to the party's executive to have the party's constitution modified to include a provision for a yearly leadership-review vote. The voting would, however, be restricted to sitting Conservative MPs. To be declared the winner of this review, a candidate would need a 15 per cent margin over his or her nearest rival. Heath had sized up his caucus and was quite sure that no single MP would be able to muster the necessary margin to defeat him. Should the 15 per cent margin of victory not be achieved, a second ballot would be held some weeks later. Thus, for the first time ever, the Tory party would hold a recorded vote for the post of party leader, a giant leap for party democracy in England.

The British Labour party has also turned to an elective system for selecting its party leader. As with the Tories, only the party's MPs are allowed to vote; however, the influence of Labour's extraparliamentary wing is very much in evidence in the final choice. The British Labour party is a very factionalized organization, with a membership that covers the political spectrum from hard-left Marxist-Leninist to centre-left liberal. Because of this diversity, attaining the position of party leader requires the support of the leaders of these factions, or, at the very least, the support of most of them.

Labour undertakes a leadership contest only when the position is vacant. Unlike the Tories, they make no provision for a leadership review, although, as was the case with former party leader Michael Foot, once the coalition of factions breaks down, the leader's position becomes untenable, and resignation soon follows. Labour's leadership process calls for a vote by all the party's sitting MPs, with two ballots, the first being a vote that includes all of the candidates, and the second a run-off between the two highest finishers in the first ballot. Despite this reliance on a vote by the party caucus, the real decision is then conveyed to the caucus members before they vote. In recent cases, the eventual winner of the caucus leadership election has also been the overwhelming choice of the extraparliamentary interest groups. Without this support, of the powerful industrial unions, for example, no leader could expect to hold power for very long, and the party's success at the polls would suffer.

Among British political parties, the Liberal Party developed the most open leadership-selection process, a type of U.S.-style primary at the national level. The party relied on an open vote of all its members in every constituency across Great Britain. The votes were tallied and weighted by constituency, according to the size of the constituency and its membership, the percentage of popular vote in the last election, and the amount of affiliation fees collected in the constituency. Thus, all the voting results were adjusted at the riding level before being tallied nationally. However, this system, devised in 1976, which led to the election of Liberal leader David Steel, did not increase interest in the Liberal Party or garner an increase in its popular vote since its inception.

Party democracy is one thing, but using it to win office is quite another. Most recently, the Liberal party has merged with the Social Democratic Party.

The Social Democrats were, before their merger with the Liberals, the other innovator in terms of leadership selection. The party was formed in 1982 with much fanfare and early promise by disgruntled members of the Labour party who objected to the power of the extraparliamentary factions, especially the Marxist-Leninist–led unions. This fear of factions led the SDP to widen the vote to all its members. Through a mail-in ballot, all party members were asked to vote for their choice for leader. The only caveats were that the potential leader had to be a sitting MP and had to win by a margin of at least 15 per cent. Again, as was the case with the Liberal Party, party democracy never translated into electoral success. In fact, what is remarkable in the British case is that the efforts to democratize leadership selection in the two smaller political parties did not lead to similar reforms in the two major parties.

The French political system is similar to that of the United States in that it provides for the direct election of both state president and the deputies for the National Assembly. As in the U.S., the party that controls the executive does not necessarily control the legislative branch of government. In fact, until the presidential and legislative elections of 1988, the French government was divided, with a Socialist president, François Mitterand, and the right-wing party in control of the National Assembly. What makes the situation even more interesting is that the French political system establishes a dual leadership of its political parties, with the president leading the party and the prime minister leading the party in the legislature. Furthermore, the prime minister can run for the post of president as the party's candidate, as occurred in 1980 and 1988 with the Rassemblement pour la République (RPR) candidate, Jacques Chirac.

French political parties of the right, especially since the Fifth Republic, are often centred on a specific political figure, like Charles de Gaulle, and therefore a certain cult of personality emerges. Such is the case with Valéry Giscard d'Estaing's Republican Party or with Chirac's RPR. The left is much less personality oriented and much more ideologically driven than the right, although one can discern a pattern of personal leadership among leftist parties.

The right-wing parties, such as the RPR and Republicans, select their leaders through meetings of the party élites. Somewhat like those held by the British Labour Party, these meetings are not limited strictly to the parties' deputies, but include leading academics, industrialists, financiers, and other members of the French upper classes who are connected with the party. In a sense, these are the faction leaders of the French right. As these parties often come together under a particular person's tutelage, that person is likely to be confirmed as party leader and will usually remain in the post for life. Once an individual withdraws from the party's leadership, the party will generally disappear, and a new coalition will emerge around the leadership of another figure. For example, Giscard's decision to pursue elective office at the local level rather than pursue another run for the presidency had made the Republican Party a dormant organization.

On the left, the Socialist Party, at present led by Mitterand, also selects its leaders through a meeting of the party élites. Like their Labour counterparts in Great Britain, French Socialists have to contend with a number of factions, ranging from centre-left to hard-left. The one major difference is that the French Socialists are largely free from the influence of the union movement, as this group is largely controlled and affiliated with the French Communist Party.

Because of this fragmentation, a number of leaders have emerged for each of these factions. The veto of any one of the factional leaders is absolute. In effect, the presidential candidate or prime minister is the party leader, but his right to lead comes from the coalition beneath him. Should the party control the national assembly and not the presidency, the prime minister becomes the de facto party leader until a presidential candidate is chosen, often the same person. If the party controls neither the presidency nor the National Assembly, an extraparliamentary apparatus made up of several of these individual faction leaders takes care of the day-to-day affairs of the party until a presidential candidate is chosen. Unlike those of the right-wing parties, the Socialist Party structure requires that the leader be a sitting deputy or president. Outside of political office, one is but a candidate, although in the Socialist Party structure, this is a position of some influence in itself.

The French Communist Party (PCF) is the other major one, although its influence beyond the labour movement has been on the wane recently. The PCF is a highly decentralized party, based on more than 25,000 individual cells. These cells are grouped together into larger federations. The party itself is controlled by a national congress, which is composed of delegates from the federations. The national congress meets to select a central committee, which in turn elects seven members to the party secretariat and to the twenty-one-member policy office. The secretariat runs the day-to-day affairs of the party, under the supervision of the national party office. The PCF's general secretary is selected by that office, based upon the support a particular individual holds within each party organization. The general secretary serves both as party leader and as the party's presidential candidate, although most of the party's operations are run by the policy office and the secretariat.

The current leader of the PCF, Georges Marchais, has led the party for most of the Fifth Republic. However, the winds of change that have blown in the Communist world have also begun to be felt in France. Marchais's once-total grasp of the party apparatus has become increasingly challenged from within. At issue are his once-open association with and enthusiastic support for many of Eastern Europe's more callous regimes, particularly his numerous visits to and staunch approval of Romanian dictator Nicolae Ceausescu. The PCF, like most Communist parties world-wide, selects its leader in a highly centralized and undemocratic way. In effect, it relies on the collusion of the leadership of the various party organizations to select a leader from among their ranks. However, once chosen, the new leader would play his supporting factions off against one another to maintain his position. Marchais, as the longest-serving Communist leader in French history, was particularly capable of demoting potential rivals and critics, thus consolidating his position at the top.

There exists a wide variety of means by which political parties select their political leaders. The United States has gone the furthest in widening the franchise, while the European parties still consider leadership selection to be a role limited to the élites. However, neither seems to offer a model of success and popular approval. In the United States, turnout for primary elections and caucuses is very low, whereas in Europe no one seems willing to contest the manner in which party leaders are elected. Furthermore, when criticism does emerge, in the United States as in Europe, the central point is the same — that regardless of which process is utilized to select political party leaders, it seems inevitably to be controlled by the party élites.

6

STANFIELD AND CLARK

In Canada, the rules have changed in the past twenty years, but the results have not always reflected the spirit behind the rules. One way or another, the party executive at the local and riding levels exercises overwhelming influence over the selection of delegates. The leader is not chosen by a democratic act of the grass-roots membership at large.

Unfortunately, the efforts to widen democratic power have also brought new abuses, such as delegate-selection meetings packed with unqualified people. For the media, such abuses make better stories than the ordinary events of conventional riding meetings. The growth in the influence of the media was the other major change ushered in by the 1967 leadership race. Television had little influence on Diefenbaker's selection as leader in 1956, but by 1967 it was present in most Canadian homes. Once again the experience of the United States spilled over into Canada. To paraphrase Marshall McLuhan, the medium became the message as the candidates in the 1967 and 1976 leadership races grew much more aware of the power of the media, especially television, the "cool medium," which could be manipulated. Candidates' speeches were now packaged for the eleven o'clock news rather than for the audience sitting before the podium.

Leadership campaigns were built around television-news deadlines, with candidates attempting to package their platforms so that their message would fit in a thirty-second news slot. The media played a significant role in the rise and fall of Robert Stanfield.

ROBERT STANFIELD

The 1966 challenge to John Diefenbaker's leadership, which had been orchestrated by Dalton Camp, left the party divided between Diefenbaker's supporters and his enemies. Diefenbaker's critics generally espoused a more radical conservative philosophy than that practised by the leader. Furthermore, the mounting influence of Western agrarianism in the formation of party policy made the rebels uneasy; as they foresaw that it would lead to an abandonment of the party by the central Canadian establishment. These two factors, coupled with some personal animosity directed at "The Chief" and his leadership style, fuelled the rebels' efforts to depose him.

The man who stepped into the leader's shoes was Robert Stanfield, a former premier of Nova Scotia. The convention that selected Stanfield was held in September 1967, and his victory, or rather Diefenbaker's embarrassing defeat in his bid to win his job back, ended the four years of open intra-party wrangling over the Chief's leadership.

Diefenbaker's problems began with the 1963 defeat of his Tory government. Under Diefenbaker, the party had gone from the largest electoral victory in Canadian history to the opposition benches, and many were ready to blame the downfall on the party leader. The election defeat brought into the open much of the discontent that had previously been kept behind the doors of the cabinet room. Soon the debate over Diefenbaker's leadership dominated every meeting of the party, from the riding level to that of national party headquarters. Dalton Camp, then president of the national Progressive Conservative Association, was the major force behind the leadership challenge. Camp engineered the campaign for a reappraisal of the leadership. After a deeply divisive internal conflict, the 1966 annual meeting of the party directed the National Executive to call a leadership convention before the end of 1967. The vote for a leadership convention was, in effect, a vote for non-confidence against Diefenbaker.

There were nine contenders for the PC leadership in 1967. Besides Diefenbaker and Stanfield, the field also included the former Manitoba premier Duff Roblin and six members of the federal cabinet — E. Davie Fulton, George Hees, Alvin Hamilton, Wallace McCutcheon, Donald Fleming, and Michael Starr. Starr and Hamilton had waited until late in the campaign before announcing their intention to run for the leadership. Both had waited until it appeared that Diefenbaker, whom they had supported against the challenge of the dissidents, would not join the race. Both felt certain that they could count on Diefenbaker's support, but they had the rug pulled out from under them when Diefenbaker announced his intention to run for the leadership. The Chief would not go down easily.

Despite Diefenbaker's presence in the field, the race was really between Duff Roblin and Robert Stanfield. However, Roblin entered the race much later than he should have, out of consideration for Diefenbaker. To have announced his intention to run early might have been construed as a slap in the face of the former leader.

I personally supported Roblin and had conferred with him on numerous occasions before his official announcement. There were a number of reasons for my choice. The first was his ability to be understood in French. Unlike Stanfield, Roblin was well liked in Québec, and especially by Premier Daniel Johnson. Given that any future PC government would require significant support from Québec, I felt that Roblin's Québec popularity was critical to the future success of the party. Coupling this with his government's record in Manitoba and his popularity among francophone Manitobans, I was sure Roblin was a winner. Although I did have some reservations about supporting a provincial premier rather than one of my caucus colleagues, the factionalism that was evident in our parliamentary ranks convinced me that the next leader of the party would have to come from outside the Commons.

As for Robert Stanfield, his decision to run for the leadership was a surprise to many people. When asked about his intentions shortly following Diefenbaker's electoral defeat, Stanfield answered that he would "take up ski jumping" rather than run for the leadership of the federal Tories, but ultimately he did join the race. His change of heart can be partially attributed to support he was promised by the dissident faction of the party. Dalton Camp, the man behind the rebellion against the Chief, was one of the prominent figures in the Stanfield team, personally contacting people at every level of the party for pledges of support. Flora MacDonald and Gordon Fairweather encouraged me and others of their colleagues to back Stanfield. I remained uncommitted, not convinced that Stanfield had the capacity to be a victorious national leader. Stanfield's main handicap was his inability to speak French coherently. While Roblin was able to get his message across in French, thanks to carefully prepared cue cards and speeches, Stanfield was, for all intents and purposes, incomprehensible.

In April 1967, I travelled to Winnipeg to address a constituency meeting in St. Boniface. On the Saturday morning before the meeting, I met with Roblin, encouraging him to announce his intention to run as soon as possible. He told me to wait until mid-June; if he was willing to enter his name, he would let me know by then. Mid-June passed, and there was no word from Duff. I assumed that he had decided not to run.

During the summer of 1967, I organized a coast-to-coast poll of Canadians on a number of political issues. Nearly 10,000 people were questioned. Regional and national reports were prepared, printed, and distributed to delegates at the September convention.

In addition to being requested to identify the federal issues that they considered most important, people were asked, "What man or woman should be named by the PC Party as leader at the September convention?" The answers showed that there was no strong national support for any of the candidates. In addition, the respondents revealed that many of them felt left out and ignored by the nominating process.

In late August, the party held a policy conference at Montmorency, just outside Québec City. Just after the conference got under way, Roblin announced his candidacy. I pledged my support for him immediately, but I knew that we were probably too late to mount a winning campaign. A few days later, on a highly publicized swing through Québec, Roblin met only a handful of actual delegates. Even at that late date, most of the Québec delegates had not been named.

The delegate-selection meetings were being organized by the time that Roblin and Diefenbaker joined the race. Many of these meetings were being held without an adequate period of time for the candidates to raise their public profiles or to establish their stands on the issues. Delegates were being chosen who were uncommitted or had pledged to support a candidate they had not had a chance to meet and question. As in all previous leadership campaigns since the 1920s, delegate selection seemed like a mechanized process, unaffected by events on the campaign trail.

Who were these delegates who were being selected to represent the party membership in the choice of party leader? They certainly did not represent the composition of the Progressive Conservative party. Over 40 per cent of the delegates had university degrees and a full 44 per cent had a family income in excess of $15,000, which, in 1967, put them in a high-income bracket. Few delegates were union members or blue-collar workers.

Also unrepresentative of the party membership were all the *ex officio* delegates. These people had served the party either as MPS or as MPPS, presided over the youth wing or other party organizations, or worked at party headquarters of the delegates at the Toronto leadership convention. *Ex officio* delegates, representatives of what could only be termed the party élite, made up 46 per cent of the total.

The delegations from many ridings also included blow-in delegates. Although it is impossible to accurately measure their numbers, they made up a sizeable portion of the delegates from Québec. Blow-in delegates were acclaimed, rather than elected, at the riding level or nominated by the riding executive to fill delegate spots left vacant. In addition, the remaining vacancies were filled at the convention itself by convention organizers with delegates from other parts of the country. Thus it was that an alternate delegate from Northern Ontario might fill a vacancy in a delegation from east-end Montréal.

The 1967 Tory leadership convention was the first in Tory party history to be heavily bankrolled. No expense was spared by the front-runners in their cross-Canada campaign. The party executive was unprepared for this new American style of leadership campaign, and therefore had no rules in place to control the spending or ensure that all the contributions made to the candidates were fully reported.

Stanfield and Roblin battled through five ballots before Stanfield received the requisite number of votes to be declared the winner. The deciding factor in Stanfield's victory was that support he enjoyed among *ex officio* delegates and the party dissidents led by Dalton Camp. While Roblin was the most popular candidate with the majority of Tory voters, especially in Québec where both Premier Johnson and Paul Sauvé's widow endorsed him, the party brass was driving the Stanfield machine. This group had talked Stanfield into taking up the challenge of a leadership race, and it was this group that prepared the groundwork, raised the funds, and ensured the support before the lanky Nova Scotian joined the race. While the national press that gathered at the convention largely ignored the *ex officio* factor in Stanfield's victory, it was apparent to those on the floor that Roblin's defeat came at the hands of this segment of the delegates. Without calling into question Stanfield's abilities or his fine record as a legislator and premier, we can regret the fact that an unelected contingent, which made up nearly half of the assembled delegates, would undermine the working of democracy in the party's leadership-selection process.

Stanfield went on to lead the party in three elections, all of which were lost, largely because of the party's inability to make inroads in Québec. This lack of electoral success, coupled with growing unrest within the party caucus, prompted Stanfield to call it quits. A leadership convention was called for February 1976 and was to be held in Ottawa.

The 1976 Conservative leadership convention was a study in contrasts. This time, the right wing was led by Diefenbaker, a reversal of the position he held in 1967. The left wing was led by Stanfield. There were a number of candidates on each side. Jack Horner, Paul Hellyer, Claude Wagner, Sinclair Stevens, and Pat Nowlan were on the right, and Jim Gillies, Flora MacDonald, John Fraser, and Joe Clark represented the left wing of the party (the so-called Red Tories). It's hard to know where Mulroney stood.

The convention featured a contrast of styles as well as policies. For my own candidacy, I ran a low-budget, low-hype campaign, as did Clark and MacDonald. Sinclair Stevens, Claude Wagner, and Brian Mulroney ran much more expensive campaigns, with some of the money going towards big-name entertainment, refreshments, meals, and delegate accommodation. Brian Mulroney, especially, stood out in this area. Although he has steadfastly refused to divulge any details concerning the financial resources behind his first leadership run, people knowledgeable in such matters have estimated his disbursements at $300,000 or more. That Mulroney finished the race without a deficit is a testimony to his fund-raising ability.

Clark's victory on the fourth ballot was a surprise to many, "Joe who?" being a catchy phrase that would haunt him even after he became prime minister. However, Clark was not a political neophyte. He had served as MP for about three years before the leadership race and had occupied a number of important positions with the party organization. In Alberta, he had worked as principal speech writer in 1959 for Cam Kirby, the leader of the provincial Progressive Conservatives in 1958–60, and helped put together Peter Lougheed's winning leadership campaign for the Alberta PCs. He was PC National Youth Federation president and worked at PC national headquarters in 1962, helping to put the election team together. By 1967, Clark helped run Davie Fulton's leadership bid. Following that convention, Clark was asked to join the staff of Robert Stanfield's office, where he remained until 1972, when he returned to Alberta to plot his bid for the riding of Rocky Mountain, for which he was elected in 1972.

Clark began considering a run for the leadership following the 1974 election. He began scouring the country for possible supporters. Like other candidates for the leadership, he realized that Stanfield would step down before long. As early as December 1974, Clark began meeting with friends and key party insiders, trying to establish if he had a base for support. Financial considerations were also a determining factor in whether Clark would run. The 1967 PC leadership convention had been one of the most expensive in Canadian history, with more delegates assembling than ever before. Indications were that the 1976 convention would be equally expensive, in part because of the increasing reliance on media and travelling during the campaign. Since 1967, the nature of running for a party leadership had taken on the appearance and methods of a mini-presidential race, complete with whistle-stop swings through virtually every important riding in the country. Clark, who had just acquired a new home in the affluent Rockcliffe area of Ottawa, could not inject much money himself into the race, nor could he count on financial support from the business community; that support would go to other candidates in the race, especially to Brian Mulroney. If Clark was to run, he would have to run a low-key, frugal campaign in the age of mega-dollar politics.

Having received the assurance that his former boss, Peter Lougheed, would not enter the leadership race, Clark tossed his hat into the ring, a novice MP from Alberta doing battle with the party's eastern élite. Some of his advisers considered that a third- or fourth-place finish would be good for Clark's career, possibly leading to a major cabinet post if he threw his support behind the victorious candidate. Clark's main opposition would come from Flora MacDonald, whose ideological stance was similar to Clark's. In addition, the so-called Flora factor — MacDonald's personality and charisma, which drew a large number of people — would hamper Clark, who lacked a distinctive style.

Clark's campaign also lacked style. The Clark team waited until four weeks before the convention before investing in campaign posters, banners, and related materials. Meanwhile, other candidates were travelling the country in fully decked out campaign buses and were appearing on television with a backdrop of campaign posters. In their attempt to run a low-key campaign, the Clark forces were in fact underselling their candidate. In any other circumstances, such strategic miscalculations would most likely have been fatal to his leadership bid.

At the official start of the leadership race, all the candidates were asked to submit detailed financial reports to the PC National Executive. These reports tend to highlight the frugality of Clark's campaign. Clark had to rely on smaller donations than some of his opponents. At one point his campaign was so strapped for cash that some of Clark's close friends and associates had to co-sign a letter of credit for $20,000 before funds could be borrowed privately.

Aided by some favourable media coverage, Clark's campaign took off in the closing weeks of the race. The mood of the convention was decidedly right of centre. Polls taken at the convention showed that a majority of the delegates described themselves as conservative and on the right of the spectrum, while a very small percentage perceived themselves as liberal in areas such as social spending.

The main challengers for the leadership were a varied group. Paul Hellyer, the former Liberal MP, was supported by at least twenty Tory MPs as well as the Diefenbaker wing of the party. His main selling point was his parliamentary experience, and his discourse was hard-right. Jack Horner's campaign was personality oriented. Although he also occupied the right of the spectrum, his rhetoric frightened some delegates as it was perceived as too strong. Horner forces were largely based in the West and did not seem inclined to make inroads with the party's eastern élite, essential to emerge victorious. The Wagner team was also on the right of the spectrum and was perhaps the most secretive of the leadership campaigns. There was little to be learned from his campaign organizers, and throughout the campaign the former "hanging judge," as he was known in Québec, remained vague in his policy pronouncements.

Brian Mulroney's campaign was also very soft on policy, but was big on show. Perhaps more so than any other campaigners, the Mulroney team sold the person rather than the program. Mulroney, having no political experience as an elected representative, was virtually unknown to those outside the party. Therefore, Mulroney's team set out to create a public profile, an operation that had a $300,000 price tag. In the end the Mulroney strategy backfired, as delegates began questioning the substance behind the PR packaging.

The remainder of the field was split among a number of lesser-known candidates who either couldn't raise the funds for a strong campaign or had support that was too local or regional to appeal to a wide number of delegates from across the country.

By convention week, Clark had managed to raise his profile substantially; now however, the crucial stage was before him. His campaign was again cash poor at the precise time when mounting the final convention assault would require large infusions of money. Hotel rooms and office space had been booked, and as the convention approached, money would have to be found to pay for them. Clark found himself trapped by his own strategy. He had run a low-key campaign, but his resulting low profile meant that he did not garner the exposure Mulroney and Horner had. Without that exposure, delegates would be unable to gauge his possible strength at the convention and might therefore be reluctant to contribute to his campaign. In the end, Clark's campaign had to borrow the funds to stage a final convention blitz. Clark had entered the campaign with a pledge to spend only what he could raise. To keep that pledge, borrowed funds had to be repaid by the convention's end. Faced with this situation, the Clark campaign organized a nation-wide telephone blitz in the last week before the convention that netted enough to pay off all outstanding bills and loans. Clark's frugal campaign would raise and spend exactly $169,135.60, most of which had been raised in small, individual contributions of approximately $150.

One aspect of financing greatly concerned me during the leadership campaign. Under the Elections Act, individuals can contribute to party constituency associations and receive receipts for income-tax purposes. It was and is obvious to me that the intent of the act meant that monies so raised were to be directed towards constituency activities. Many leadership candidates raised money for their campaigns through their riding associations, thus giving contributors receipts for income-tax purposes. Surely this practice is a case for reform.

The two nights of the convention were to be occasions when Diefenbaker and Stanfield would be honoured, although the candidates would be able to gauge their support on the first night, when all the delegates were present in and around the Civic Centre. When the candidates were introduced, Clark received a strong ovation, but so did his main opponents. The delegate-tracking system that the Clark team had devised began to fall apart, making it impossible for Clark to find out which way some of the undecided delegates were going.

But who exactly were these delegates? As with the 1967 PC leadership convention, a disproportionate number of the 1976 delegates represented the professional élite in Canadian society. The working-class stratum was underrepresented, as usual. The majority of the delegates had post-secondary education and a gross family income above the national average. Homemakers were few in number and did not represent a cohesive voting block. In addition, as in all previous conventions, the *ex officio* contingent — MPS, MLAS, senators, riding association presidents, presidents of the youth and women's wings, party executive, and so on — was disproportionately large, this time representing over 25 per cent of the delegates. The one major difference between the 1976 and the 1967 conventions was that most Québec delegates had been selected at the riding level, rather than being blow-in delegates. The presence of two strong candidates from Québec, Mulroney and Wagner, probably explains this. Many of these Québec delegates were chosen as parts of slates organized by the Wagner and, to a lesser extent, the Mulroney forces.

Friday, February 20, day two of the convention, was the day for the policy sessions — a chance for delegates to question the leadership candidates. Many questions were planted to make one candidate look good or an opposing candidate look bad. Overall, Clark did well in the policy forums, although Brian Mulroney was also well received, especially with his stance on bilingualism.

Saturday was the crucial day at the convention, the day of the candidate speeches. Clark's team had arranged for his speech to be introduced by Allan Laakkonen, a grass-roots party worker. Laakkonen's speech began with his introducing himself as the "one who rings doorbells . . . works the committee rooms . . . and carries the signs." By having a member of the grass roots introduce his speech to the convention, Clark was able to enhance his populist image while the other delegates only emphasized their associations with the backroom élite by relying on introductions from the party's establishment. In the draw that allocated the order of the speeches, Clark came out fifth, a good position, in the middle of the pack. He would speak after MacDonald, but before many of the harder-line candidates, such as Hellyer and Wagner.

Clark entered the Civic Centre arena on Saturday afternoon in an antique landau as his campaign's brass band played the campaign's theme song. The whole effect was one of sleekness, an effort to show that if they chose to, the Clark team could outperform the Mulroney forces at their own game. Clark's speech, however, did not go well; it was too long and lacking in excitement. To make things worse, Wagner and MacDonald spoke compellingly.

Clark's speech had been geared towards raising support among the Québec delegates, and to this end, a fair portion of it was delivered in French. This effort would reduce his image as a Western anglophone and place him among the bilingual candidates — me, Mulroney, and Wagner. In addition, by enhancing the bilingual aspect, Clark hoped to be perceived as a possible winner in the next federal election where the party would need the Québec vote to win.

Sunday was voting day. The first ballot's results would finally settle the question of the accuracy of the delegate tracking that all the campaigns had been running throughout the race. The Clark team was expecting 300 votes on the first ballot, and when the results were announced and he had only 277, many in his camp thought it was all over. However, Clark had expected fourth place on the first ballot and he found himself third, and the leading candidate from outside Québec. The sombre mood in the Clark camp changed as delegates began moving to his section in the Civic Centre. First, James Gillies and I moved over to the Clark camp. My delegates, plus Gillies's, potentially added 120 votes to Clark's total for the second ballot. Then, to everyone's surprise, Sinclair Stevens pledged his support for Clark, adding a potential 182 votes. Stevens had been identified with the right wing of the party, and his support for Clark was a turning point. If Stevens could support Clark, then a number of other right-of-centre delegates could consider Clark as the best alternative candidate around whom to build a coalition of the various party factions for the next election.

The second-ballot results had Clark second only to Wagner. Clark received 532 votes, Wagner 667, and Mulroney finished third, with 419. The next round of withdrawals would be critical. As expected, MacDonald made her way to Clark's box, while Horner was moving over to Wagner's box. Mulroney was positive that there would be a fourth ballot and chose to stay in. Either way, his support would have sealed the convention's conclusion.

The third-ballot results still had Clark second to Wagner, 969 to 1,003, with Mulroney losing support and dropping to 369. Mulroney still elected to stay in for the fourth ballot. He had no chance of victory but was not damaging his position within the party by siding with one or the other of his opponents. Despite this, many of Mulroney's supporters went over to Clark. Ideologically, they were closer to Clark than to Wagner.

Clark's team knew they had won by the look on the faces of Claude Wagner and his wife. The results had been leaked to them, and their downcast expressions said it all. Clark, who had been sitting in his box, working on his victory speech (he had never made allowances for defeat), was cheered loudly when the results were announced. He had won by sixty-five votes, one of the smallest margins of victory ever.

Although the nature of leadership contests has changed in the age of television and nation-wide campaigning, the rules have not.

Since 1967, the cost of running for a party leadership has spiralled as more reliance is placed on technology, delegate tracking, polling, and air travel. The two big M's — media exposure and money — have limited the importance and contributions of the lesser-known and less well-financed candidates. This trend may be working against our ideal of truly representative democratic gatherings for the purpose of leadership selection.

Consider as well that Dief, Stanfield, and Clark were eventually forced out of their jobs by party élites. The majority of the delegates at leadership conventions are members of an élite group, not ordinary Canadians. These are the people who elected Clark and who later got rid of him. Thus, we must address this very important point: do we want a broad base of Canadians at the grass-roots level included in the process of leadership selection? If so, we must change the traditional system so as to include the party rank and file. This means inclusion not just at the riding level, where our system of delegate selection fails them, but right up to the final decision.

7

THE FALL OF CLARK AND THE RISE OF MULRONEY

Between 1958 and 1962, while John Diefenbaker presided over a majority Progressive Conservative government, a number of bright young men who would play important roles in Canada were drawn to Ottawa. I have a clear recollection of some of the assistants who worked in ministers' offices. There were Michael Pitfield and Marc Lalonde, who came to help Justice Minister Davie Fulton. There was Brian Mulroney, a student at that time, who worked in the office of Alvin Hamilton, then minister of Agriculture, as a special assistant. I also remember many visits to the Hill by Joe Clark, who was then active with the Young Conservatives. Little did I realize at the time that I was meeting a future clerk of the Privy Council, a future minister of Finance, and two future prime ministers.

During the 1962 federal election campaign, Alvin Hamilton visited my home riding to address a group of English-speaking farmers. His young assistant accompanied him. Mulroney must have circulated among the constituents that evening, because I have in my files a letter that he wrote to one of them. The letter seems to show potential in public service, a readiness to respond to an individual's needs and

89

to provide whatever service or information his access to ministry resources could.

Despite the ability he might have had for serving and charming constituents, Mulroney did not do most of his party work at a grass-roots level. At a very young age, he had the ear of Diefenbaker. He would later establish equally good relations with Stanfield. His particular service to the party was most often rendered through his skill at fund-raising activities. He played a major part in organizing fund-raising dinners for the party in Montréal at regular intervals. This work undoubtedly served his career by bringing him into contact with corporate leaders.

Because of the influence they would have on Mulroney's career, the character of the old-guard Montréal Tory establishment to which some of those corporate leaders belonged is important to consider. Even though our party was officially named the Progressive Conservative Party in 1942 in order to accommodate John Bracken and the Western Progressive Movement, many old-time, right-wing Tories never took the "Progressive" label very seriously. When the ex-premier of Ontario, Col. George Drew, became party leader in 1948, the party truly took on an added conservative flavour. At that time, the Progressive Conservative Party was virtually nonexistent in Québec. The Tories who did exist among the Montréal establishment had to be seen to be believed. One of them said to me in that period that they might have nominated Diefenbaker because of his fighting qualities, but the name "Diefenbaker" would never do to take to the electorate. Only upon Drew's imminent retirement did I consider joining a party that I felt could be uniquely Canadian in being *progressive*, civilized, decent, and humane in social policy, while simultaneously being conservative in economic policy. I took the full name "Progressive Conservative" seriously, feeling that if we could transform the traditional Tory party along those lines, we could widen its electoral appeal and credibility. For me, there has never been any inconsistency in being progressive in social policy and conservative in economic policy. The two notions are in no way mutually exclusive, as liberals and socialists would have us believe.

I first met Mulroney at my home in Knowlton, when he came with Alvin Hamilton in 1962, and it would not be an exaggeration to state that already we were approaching the political process from different directions. In 1962, Mulroney was making his first moves to get on side with the Montréal Tories. At that time, I was putting down roots in a rural, small-town, largely francophone riding across the St. Lawrence River from Montréal. While it was just a few miles away from the city, my riding was in another world from that inhabited by the people Mulroney was cultivating in Montréal. One acquaintance in the city's Tory circles pleaded with me to run in "an important West Island riding," as opposed to getting lost in the hinterland. There's an irony in all this, as I truly feel Mulroney has progressive social-policy instincts but, in going for the leadership and overthrowing Clark, he relied heavily on old-line traditional Tory Conservatives, conservatives who would tie his hands in the future.

I felt that Mulroney and his Montréal group had a certain detachment, almost disdain, for day-to-day political work at the constituency level and for the workers who toiled in those fields. They were tacticians, officers who directed the efforts of lower-ranking workers. By the time I was named minister of state for Social Programmes in 1979, I was publicly critical of the Montréal party generals. Mulroney was aware of my criticisms, but hardly abashed by them.

Elected representatives were held in such low regard by this group that we were sometimes forgotten altogether. Mulroney and his friends arranged a fund-raising dinner at the

Queen Elizabeth Hotel some months before the 1979 election. A number of speeches and activities had been organized, but Roch LaSalle and I, the only two elected representatives from the Province of Québec, were overlooked. Only after intervention from people of Clark's group did Brian arrange to have us introduced to the audience at an appropriate time.

Mulroney seems to share an opinion with Trudeau, who claimed that members of Parliament became nobodies once they had left Parliament Hill. Mulroney did not seem to feel it inappropriate that he should seek the party leadership without ever having held elective office. It was Mulroney and his group who advocated using a $300,000 hand-out to coax Claude Wagner, the ex-judge and ex–Liberal MPP, to join the Tory caucus, thus inflicting him on Stanfield and the Québec electorate. His nomination of his old college friend Lucien Bouchard to the post of secretary of state enraged Mulroney's elected caucus, who have been shown that their work on behalf of constituents and their party counts for little. Like his boss, Bouchard had avoided the inconvenience of seeking election before being awarded a post of significant political power.

For the past couple of decades, the roles of the party caucus and elected members of Parliament have diminished in direct proportion to the rise in power of the extraparliamentary wing of the party. In the television age, the longer elected officials remain elected, the more negative baggage they normally accumulate. Mulroney would later capitalize on this unfortunate phenomenon in a city where there were no elected Progressive Conservative members, where the party power brokers never attempted to conceal their contempt for those who managed to get elected. I was not always faking when I quipped that my greatest sin against the party establishment in Québec was that I got elected.

Mulroney and his group showed little sign of their later ability to sweep Québec during the Clark years. The time span between the convention in February 1976 and the election of 1979 should have been a period of rebuilding for the Conservatives in Québec, but it was not. At the convention, Clark had received more support from Québec than any of the other candidates from outside the province. And Clark's view of the country and his stand on major issues should have been acceptable to most Quebeckers. The constitutional debate had become polarized between the separatist option of René Lévesque and Trudeau's total faith in centralized federal authority. Like Trudeau's colleague and old friend Gérard Pelletier, Clark articulated an acceptable and viable middle option between the two constitutional extremes.

I believe Clark's lack of success was partly attributable to the paucity of cooperation from the Mulroney and Wagner camps. Never a team player, Wagner treated his younger leader with haughty indifference. Realizing that Clark would not repeat Stanfield's mistake of appointing a Québec lieutenant, Wagner was ripe for picking by the Liberals. When Trudeau tempted him with an offer, Wagner was quick to swallow the bait. While Trudeau gave Jack Horner a cabinet post to lure him across the floor, he could hardly do the same for Wagner. Wagner had already switched parties once in recent history. The solution that Trudeau found to get Wagner out of his seat in the Commons was to appoint him to the Senate.

Trudeau was using the tools he had available to try to eliminate PC representation from the political map of Québec. A number of his emissaries came to visit me in my West Block office, ostensibly for a friendly chat, but more precisely to see if, after twenty years of hard fighting, I wouldn't welcome a comfortable seat in the Red Chamber. They soon got my answer. I have never hidden my distaste for the Canadian Senate. Whatever potential for useful activity the Senate might have had in the original scheme of things has been sabotaged by the cynicism of successive prime ministers. I would draw welfare rather than sit or sleep in the Red Chamber. The young Canadians who have gone there in the past few years, sacrificing whatever other potential they might have had for real service to the Canadian public, should be ashamed of themselves.

Senate reform is a great topic of conversation these days. Every time I hear it discussed, I am reminded of work I used to do among prison inmates in years gone by. I went into my work with my rose-coloured glasses in place. Soon I realized that certain hard-core criminals, albeit a small percentage, could not be reformed or rehabilitated under present conditions. Maybe in the future we shall have techniques that will return them safely to society, but not now. It is thus with the Canadian Senate. I believe it is beyond redemption and cannot be saved.

There are those who talk about an elected Senate, a triple-E Senate, with real powers. We might ask, where will this reformed Senate get its newfound powers — by provincial or federal authority? What happens if the Senate is controlled by one party and the Commons by another? It is fair to say that in the United States, the Senate can be controlled by one party and the House by another. Yet, our southern neighbours have conscientiously advocated separation of powers in their constitutional framework. Under our system of *responsible parliamentary* government, having a Senate controlled by one party and the House by another would spell *chaos*. In the unlikely event that we abolish our parliamentary system, under a new constitution things might be different. I have heard it said again and again that senators go to Ottawa to give legislation emanating from the Commons a sober second look. I chuckle to myself when I hear that, and am reminded of my first look at the Senate and its inhabitants soon after my election in 1958.

As a young man in Montréal, like anybody else, I had to attend funerals. Joseph Wray had a fine funeral home on Mountain Street in the middle of the city. It has now been converted into a disco. Wray's catered to what my grandmother often referred to as the "carriage trade." I have a clear recollection of Wray's. We all know that the sense of smell can evoke instant memories of things past. My grandmother wore a certain perfume. Thirty years later, when I smell on another lady the brand of perfume she wore, I can see her in my mind's eye. It was thus with Wray's funeral parlour and the Canadian Senate. When entering Wray's, I would invariably smell a mixture of flowers and the oak panels of the chapel. When I was first ushered into the Senate for royal assent to bills emanating from the House, I would see flowers arranged in the Senate lobby. As at Wray's, much oak was used in its construction. Instant recall went into operation as I sniffed the same combination of flowers and oak. There was one big difference. Here, the corpses were not in caskets. Sitting and slumbering with their eyes shut and their heads hanging over their upper bodies, the aged senators were the embodiment of Shakespeare's seventh age: "All the world's a stage and . . . And one man in his time plays many parts; his acts being seven ages."

In all fairness, I did find the Senate useful on at least one occasion during my parliamentary career. When attending the United Nations as a delegate in 1958, I wanted to see the New York Yankees play in the World Series. This desire prompted me to write a letter on Commons stationery to the Yankees' front office, asking for Series tickets. Ten days went by, and I had no answer. I was about to give up when I got a brain wave. Senators are powerful and important people in the United States. It came to mind that officials at the Yankees' front office would not differentiate between the importance of senators on this and on the other side of the border. So I dictated a letter, this time on Senate stationery, and had a reluctant senator sign it. The letter was delivered by courier, and the very next day a messenger arrived with the tickets. The only problem was, the senator wanted some of them. I got to keep the rest.

While I feel the Senate should be abolished under parliamentary rules, I am not averse to an elected Senate, as long as those advocating it are willing to scrap the parliamentary system of responsible government for a presidential system based on the separation of powers. Imagine, under our parliamentary system, a Conservative-dominated House of Commons with a Liberal-dominated elected Senate. The ensuing deadlock would be indescribable. An elected Senate would be all right under a presidential system, which very possibly will be the hallmark of our new constitution. When it comes to choosing leaders, and in our approach to many of our government institutions, Canadians often flirt with the presidential approach. This ambiguity invariably gives us the worst of both worlds regarding the presidential and parliamentary systems of government.

During Clark's early stewardship of the party, Mulroney sulked conspicuously on the sidelines. One indication of this involved a meeting Clark convened in the leader's boardroom in the Centre Block of the Parliament Buildings, soon after his nomination as leader. The purpose of the meeting was to arrange a formula whereby the national party would assist all defeated leadership candidates to meet their campaign deficits. All candidates had agreed to disclose the sources of their funds in an open and honest way. Mulroney did not turn up at the meeting and refused to disclose the source of his funds, as agreed. A *Financial Post* article that appeared in June 1978 quoted Mulroney as saying, "If Joe Clark wins this election, I'll eat this plate. I mean, let's look at it. Can you see any way he can win?

Any way at all?" Mulroney was confident that he could provide the party with the kind of leadership that would be much more attractive to voters. Still, he did not run in the 1979 election.

At a caucus meeting following the publication of the article, several MPS referred to it. I warned Clark that he would face the same fate that had overtaken Diefenbaker and Stanfield if he didn't publicly demand party loyalty and discipline. Clark just asked us to keep our cool and expressed no public annoyance at Mulroney.

While we went on to form a minority government after the 1979 campaign, once again the party was routed in Québec. We should have done better there. Joe was doing his best, but he had elected to work with the same old gang, and they had produced the same old results.

We might have done better. Trudeau was more popular than the Liberal Party, but many people voted for the leader, not the party. Still, a strong grass-roots campaign might have changed the results in some ridings. Instead, some Montréal organizer took a totally inexplicable tack. He leaked to the press a list of ridings the party had written off as hopeless — ridings where sincere candidates were working long hours to break through the Liberals' thick red line.

Then there was the province-wide ad campaign. As the election campaign drew to a close, somebody dreamed up the idea of a TV spot ad showing Trudeau in prison, with his hands gripping the bars. A loud voice-over cited all the crimes of his Liberal government, and the prime minister was pronounced guilty (*coupable*). Even party supporters angrily denounced the advertisement as being not only negative but in extremely poor taste.

Election day showed that the Québec team had let the party down again. With a reasonable showing in Québec, Clark could have formed a majority government and possibly have named more elected cabinet ministers from Québec. I was one of two members elected from Québec. I had won my own riding with a comfortable majority and was sworn in as minister of state for Social Programmes. Yet, we were painfully aware of how underrepresented we were in this politically crucial province. Trudeau had used patronage appointments very effectively in promoting his political objectives. It is now common knowledge that Clark had little interest in the discretionary patronage appointments that were in his power to disperse. There was the case of Guy Charbonneau, a Montréal insurance broker, who had done an excellent job as a fund-raiser in Québec. Clark did not consider this an adequate reason to appoint Charbonneau to the Canadian Senate, but Mulroney and his associates read the riot act and the appointment went through.

Québec patronage appointments continued to be an issue between Joe Clark and the Québec party organization. It surfaced late in the summer of 1979 at a cabinet meeting at the Château Frontenac in Québec City. We had long and good working sessions. Whoever believed the "wimp" label sometimes hung on Clark had not witnessed his solid and creative handling of cabinet. On the last day of the meetings, we were informed that the Québec City regional organization had prepared a luncheon for us. We were to find that the lunch was bait for an ambush.

Clark had neglected to make any significant discretionary appointments, except for Senator Arthur Tremblay, who had been a senior mandarin during the Lesage years. Daniel Johnson and his followers had long called for Tremblay's head, but to no avail. Joe was apparently impressed, not by his service to the blue machine, but by his credentials as a constitutional expert. I have often met people with strong points of view on our Canadian constitution, but I'm not sure how one defines an expert in that field. The boys from

Québec were not looking for that kind of qualification for patronage appointments. At the luncheon, they attacked his lack of support for their efforts. Clark sat red faced. His handling of patronage matters, no matter how distasteful they were to him, proved to be a large part of Clark's undoing. "To the victors belong the spoils" didn't play well as a tune in the Clark repertoire.

During nine months in office, Clark made only approximately 150 Tory appointments — ten were senators. When the government fell in December 1979, a list of 153 appointments was awaiting approval. Clark said they were meant to be Christmas presents, but now they were frozen because of defeat. Mulroney would eventually profit from this state of affairs, as he had a more pragmatic attitude to the use of rewards and would exploit it to the full. During his climb to the leadership in 1983, he pulled out all the stops on the issue and severely wounded Clark by making it abundantly clear that a Mulroney-led government would look after the faithful.

While Clark is, in so many ways, warm, civilized, and sincere, I feel he has an innate shyness that discouraged him, when he was the Conservative leader, from reaching out to "stroke" his supporters. Stroking and keeping in touch with the faithful are critically important in politics, and Clark largely neglected this important part of his role. A phone call, letter, or pat on the back from a party leader helps keep party workers enthusiastic. Politicians and political workers need recognition and encouragement. Long periods of silence from the leader lower morale. Clark was guilty of omission in this area. Mulroney, like former president Lyndon Johnson, is a telephone junkie. He knows how to use the telephone to buoy up the troops and bolster morale.

The summer months of 1979 skipped by before we knew it. There was loud press and public criticism over the fact that we had gone through the summer months without facing Parliament and convening the House. Clark and his ministers were getting their feet under their desks. With the exception of the brief Diefenbaker interlude, the Grits had been in power for almost forty years. Much work was to be done. While our transition to power was better than during the Diefenbaker years, it wasn't easy, and as we made our plans to meet Parliament, there were few concrete results for people to see. I knew that we needed a more substantial legislative agenda.

What happened next would soon open the door for Mulroney and his supporters. While Clark's handling of his cabinet and government matters in general must be given high marks, he had flaws that would prove fatal. Each morning the prime minister would meet with his non-elected staff, much as does the president of the United States. Often, to the resentment of able elected cabinet officers, these men start to wield enormous power and influence. Henry Kissinger wrote of his White House years that frequently those who had most helped the president get elected were the least equipped to help him govern. Joe's non-elected advisers were about to get him into trouble.

Two major events helped cripple the Clark government, one orchestrating its fall in the House and ultimate defeat at the polls in February of 1980. They were the attempted privatization of Petro-Canada and the eighteen-cent tax on gas at the pumps. Cabinet briefings on Petro-Canada and proposed privatization reminded me of *Alice's Adventures in Wonderland*.

Sometimes when we listen to modern contemporary music, look at modern art or hear readings of modern poetry, we pretend to appreciate and understand these offerings at first exposure. I well remember attending symphony concerts when a contemporary piece was played for the first time. At intermission, the audience would gather in the lobby. "How did you like it?" one listener would ask another. "Oh, I found it very interesting!" would be a normal reply. Interesting was one thing. Understanding, love, and, appreciation would only come after repeated listening.

Cabinet briefings on Petro-Canada by the bureaucracy reminded me of looking at abstract art for the very first time. Reserving judgement in the hope of future understanding and appreciation was the order of the day. Bureaucratic gobbledegook and flow charts left me dazed. While the cabinet broke for refreshment breaks during the briefing, everybody feigned interest, but nobody pretended to understand the implications of the convoluted presentation by officials from Energy, Mines and Resources. In the end, Clark virtually became his own Energy minister, while officials in the department remained in their exotic dream world. Soon he would be in open warfare with Peter Lougheed, the premier of Alberta, over energy policy that in effect never really got off the drawing board. We were to blame, but ministers found it impossible to defend a policy when departmental briefings were so horrendously deficient and overly complicated. The government was wounded.

The crisis was precipitated by John Crosbie, then minister of Finance. Brilliant as he was, he was also proud and stubborn. Because of budget secrecy, cabinet ministers were not aware of the budget provisions. We should have seen the problems in the provision to tax gas eighteen cents per gallon at the pump. Crosbie was about to play Russian roulette with the government's future. His budget of short-term pain for long-term gain constituted an act of political masochism. Because of budget secrecy, we were in trouble before we knew it.

On the morning of December 14, 1979, after a motion was moved by Bob Rae of the NDP, my executive assistant, Brian Derrick, informed me that there was a strong rumour on Parliament Hill that the combined opposition would attempt to defeat us on a vote of non-confidence that evening. By that time, I knew we were in trouble as the political implications of the eighteen-cent gas increase were hitting us, but I felt little need to worry. Surely, Clark would act and enable us to survive, even if we were in a minority situation.

Clark could have saved the day had he wanted to. He didn't make that effort. It is reported that the leadership qualities Clark displayed with his cabinet colleagues at the cabinet table were lacking during his meeting with non-elected officials. At these latter meetings, he often seemed lost, as if he found it hard to sort out the issues. How else can we explain what happened that day?

Clark's non-elected advisers didn't believe the opposition would go to the limit in the House to defeat us. He had seriously underestimated the cunning, intrigue, and ability of the Liberal House leader, Allan MacEachen. After all, Trudeau had announced his retirement and merely sat like a bearded ghost in the Commons, refusing to carry out his constitutional duties as opposition leader. While dissolving the House and calling an election are solely the responsibility of the prime minister, I assumed Clark would sound out his cabinet colleagues on this issue. My assumption was wrong. He chose to closet himself with the non-elected officials, completely detached from the realities of grass-roots public opinion. They compared circumstances at that time with those surrounding the Diefenbaker minority government when it went to the people in 1958. The move had worked well for Diefenbaker, but our situation was different. The comparison was seriously flawed.

We had no legislative record to go to the people with, as had Diefenbaker twenty-two years before when he dissolved the House and let his minority government face the people. Diefenbaker had been far ahead in the polls with an excellent minority-government legislative agenda already completed. We had, in December 1979, completed no such agenda and were more than 10 per cent behind in the polls.

Diefenbaker was in control of the House and dissolved it. Clark, as prime minister, would be forced into an election after being defeated in the House.

There was an additional factor that influenced Clark's feeling. The prime minister realized that many tough economic decisions would have to be made by the government and felt that cooperating with the NDP in a minority situation would be futile. He wanted to clear the air and go to the people. It was in this spirit that he entered the House at 8:00 that evening. All of his cabinet colleagues were in the dark, and by the time the House convened, we were individually and collectively concerned, gathering and talking in small groups on the floor of the House. The prime minister just sat in his seat, seemingly unperturbed by it all. As is the custom before all votes, the Whip gave Walter Baker, our House leader, the head count. We were going down. There weren't enough PCs present for the vote. Baker had done his job as best he could. The press later contrived to blame Baker directly or indirectly for the ensuing calamity, but he was merely the messenger, and I assume his message was delivered. It was still not too late to act. The prime minister could have stalled for time and could have had his House leader announce a change in the order of House business to permit us to gather our forces and postpone the election.

Clark did not act to save the government. The bells stopped ringing. The vote was taken. We went down to defeat on prime-time television before an incredulous public. Clark dissolved the House and went to the people. Clark and his advisers felt the public would bury the Liberals on election day for forcing an election. That sentiment did, in fact, last for a while early on in the campaign, but soon public opinion turned against a government that had held power but allowed a weak and rudderless opposition to force them into an election.

As Clark's grip gradually slipped — first by losing in the 1980 general election in March, and then by capitulating at the party meeting in Winnipeg after nearly 70 per cent of those attending the meeting voted to endorse his leadership — the stage was set for Mulroney. The fact that he had never held an elective office would count for little as long as there were no truly democratic rules in place regarding leadership funding and leadership-convention delegate selection. A sizeable section of the parliamentary caucus had swung against Clark. Even so, in the winter of 1983, most of the power and influence rested with the extraparliamentary wing of the party. This was Mulroney's base of power. Added to that, Mulroney had long since had his hands on important segments of the party fund-raising apparatus. Lots of money — the sinews of political war — would be at his disposal.

Mulroney's eventual rise to power at the Ottawa convention in June 1983 can be said to be based on a number of factors. First of all, there was the increasing power of the extraparliamentary membership itself. Mulroney's initial power base was in the city of Montréal, where, as already stated, there were no Progressive Conservative members of Parliament. The coterie of establishment party people that surrounded Mulroney on the Island of Montréal had, and still have, a historical disdain for elected members of Parliament. Mulroney capitalized on this and helped mobilize the sentiment. Then there was the phenomenon of "anybody but Clark." Although Clark received support at the party's annual meeting in Ottawa, he was still having great trouble leading the caucus, and a substantial and growing number within the caucus were dissatisfied with his leadership.

Some of Mulroney's backers tried to get Clark to call a leadership contest after the 1981 general meeting in Ottawa, where Joe got 66.4 per cent of the vote supporting him. Clark refused, realizing that he had two years to go before Winnipeg, and that a large proportion of the vote against him hinged on the fact that he had recently lost power and that he had let his minority government fall in 1980.

The two years after the 1981 general meeting in Ottawa were filled with frenzied activity on the part of Mulroney supporters. It seemed that the Ritz Carlton Hotel in Montréal, where Mulroney was a director, became an unofficial headquarters for his leadership campaign. The hotel was situated a stone's throw from where Mulroney had his offices as president and chief executive officer of the Iron Ore Company of Canada. Had Joe Clark opted to keep in touch with some of his closest friends and supporters, he would have been aware of what was going on. Perhaps, deep down, he was, but if so, he made an odd decision when he agreed to meet with Mulroney at the Ritz Carlton on December 6, 1982, not much over a month before the meeting was to be held in Winnipeg. As I watched the TV reporting that day, I felt sick. There was poor Joe, crowded into a room at the Ritz beside Mulroney. The room was jammed full of Mulroney's supporters. While I looked at the television coverage, I saw Mulroney put his arm on Joe's shoulder as he said, "He's my leader. He always will be." I was perfectly aware that the Mulroney forces were out, with plenty of cash, establishing their plans to overthrow Clark once the Winnipeg convention got under way. Mulroney knew it too, and to see Joe there, in enemy territory for him, supposedly believing Mulroney's pledge of allegiance, was painful to me.

Later, at a weekend meeting of the Québec party, the national president, Peter Blaikie, had a confrontation with the Mulroney supporters, saying that they were attempting to take control of the party in Québec. This time, the Mulroney forces won every post on the Québec executive.

Mulroney, because of the Ritz Carlton meeting, felt he had distanced himself from his supporters, who were moving to overthrow Clark in Winnipeg. If I had ever had any doubts about Mulroney's intentions, they were dissipated in late January 1983, once I boarded the Air Canada jet taking me from Dorval Airport in Montréal to Winnipeg. Mulroney and his wife, Mila, boarded the plane just before me, accompanied by a coterie of supporters. On the way out to Winnipeg, I sat in the front of the plane. At one point, Mulroney came forward and sat beside me, ostensibly just to have a general chat about the prospective proceedings at Winnipeg. He made absolutely no attempt to hide his contempt for Clark, and it was obvious what he had in mind. In Winnipeg, things were programmed to go wrong for Joe.

At the Winnipeg meeting, Clark got approximately the same support that he had received two years previously, at the Ottawa convention. Incredible as it might seem, Clark felt this was not enough and called a leadership convention. This move merely added to my belief that deep down, in his subconscious, Clark really didn't want to lead the party or be prime minister. It seemed to me that the support he got was ample to allow him to carry on. By capitulating, he was opening the door to his eventual demise. In all fairness to Clark, there were other factors at work. Undoubtedly he did not want to carry on without the majority support of his caucus, which he knew he did not have. Mulroney supporters within the caucus had been active over the past number of months.

Two members of Parliament, Elmer MacKay and Chris Speyer, among others, organized a letter-writing campaign within the caucus. Individual members who did not want to write directly to Clark, telling him to quit, gave sealed letters to MacKay and his group, letters indicating they had withdrawn their support from the leader. These letters would be made public if and when a majority of the caucus had turned against the leader, and he would not quit under certain circumstances, those being that Clark should obtain an as yet undetermined percentage of the vote in Winnipeg. Friends of Clark, such as Harvie André of Calgary, told him that the caucus uprising was not significant, but this was incorrect.

Sometime before the Winnipeg meeting, the caucus had to elect a chairman. Bill McKnight was Clark's choice, and Ron Huntington was supported by the anti-Clark faction. Huntingdon won out. While the extraparliamentary wing of the party would largely support Clark at Winnipeg, the caucus proved to be a major factor in his downfall. Clark's error, it could be argued, was in insisting he have 70 per cent of the vote.

I happened to be outside the main convention hall on the first day of the proceedings when I witnessed Mulroney in an angry confrontation with the national press. One of his supporters, Jean-Yves Lortie, had showed up with two separate cheques amounting to $56,000, in order to register two hundred Québec delegates *"en bloc."* The practice was that delegates from across the country were meant to be registered individually before the convention got under way. Mulroney was virtually having a temper tantrum under the television lights, saying that the Québec delegation was being "abused and humiliated by grossly overpaid party bureaucrats." All that was really happening was the Credentials Committee chief, MP Scott Fennell, held up their registration while their individual credentials were being verified. Mulroney termed this treatment "unforgivable, disgusting in the extreme."

The Sunday morning after Clark had made his dramatic announcement that he would call a leadership convention, I met briefly with him, and at the same time pledged my support. Quite frankly, I was faced with a dilemma. Much of the party was angry at Clark for losing power the way he did, and I must say I shared these sentiments.

Between mid-February and early March, it became apparent that Mulroney was getting ready to declare his leadership bid. To his intimates and some key members of the press corps, he let it be known what his intentions were. By this time, Mulroney had approximately a dozen full-time workers toiling in an office on de Lorimier Avenue in Montréal, and on March 9, a "Friends of Brian Mulroney Dinner" was organized in the ballroom of Montréal's Queen Elizabeth Hotel. Keith Morgan, one of Mulroney's key supporters, had played a large role in organizing it. On March 21, 1983, the day after he had gone to Sept-Iles for a farewell meeting with employees of Iron Ore Company of Canada, the company he headed for seven years, he officially announced his campaign for the party leadership. John Crosbie also announced his candidacy on that day.

The 1983 leadership campaign was extremely controversial in the way it was waged. The delegate-selection meeting in Brome–Missisquoi, described earlier, was but one example of the tricks that were used. In Longueuil, a Clark partisan succeeded in having Mulroney's official representatives barred from the delegate-selection meeting.

In the Montréal riding of St. Jacques, twenty voters from a men's hostel were bussed to a meeting by Mulroney supporters. The men flashed copies of Old Brewery Mission identification cards to receive their ballots. Asked about the presence of the men from the hostel, a Mulroney organizer said, "They're very conscientious electors. I hope there'll be some beer for them later." Sure enough, when the ballots were counted and Mulroney's slate had won by twenty-seven votes, cases of beer were carted out from the hall's kitchen.

Mulroney supporters complained of attempts to mislead would-be voters in Verchères riding by giving them false information about the date of the meeting. In the riding of Don Valley East, Koreans, Greeks, and Italians, signed as new Tory party members, voted in blocs for Clark at the delegate-selection meeting. Joe Clark's summary of the campaign might have been intended for his political tombstone. "Democracy is sometimes messy," he said to a reporter a few days before the convention.

About the end of May, in Edmonton, an agent from Mulroney's campaign, along with the agents of four other candidates, began discussing a deal to beat Clark. At that time, the so-called anybody-but-Clark strategy was thrashed out. Mulroney had travelled almost 40,000 miles and had visited nearly all the federal ridings from coast to coast. Learning from his 1976 bid for power, he made a determined effort to play down any outward show of extravagance. By the time the convention opened in Ottawa on the weekend starting June 10, 1983, the die had pretty much been cast.

I sat with Joe Clark and his family and with other former leadership candidates for the party, including Bob Stanfield and Duff Roblin, and at the end of nine hours and four ballots in intense heat at the crowded Ottawa Civic Centre, Mulroney downed Clark by 1,584 votes to 1,325. It was exactly 9:20 p.m. on Saturday, June 11, 1983, when Mulroney was declared the victor.

In the convention hall, national television caught me in a very private moment, looking sad, with my head in my hands. It was partly fatigue and partly a deep sense of sympathy for Joe Clark and his family beside me in the box. It was surely from a realization that my high-school dream and parliamentary career had come to an end with Mulroney as the new party leader, a leader who had never held elective office and about whom I had the most profound misgivings.

8

RECOMMENDATIONS FOR REFORM
"ONE MEMBER — ONE VOTE"

We have seen the evolution of the leadership-selection process in Canada since Confederation. Initially, the Governor General had great influence in the selection of our party leaders, at times consulting his colleagues in England on choices for the colonies. As the Governor General's influence waned, the cabinet then constituted the forum in which party leaders and prime ministers were selected. Soon thereafter, the stamp of approval from the party caucus became a virtual necessity. As we moved into the twentieth century, the extraparliamentary wings of our parties made their influence felt in the selection of leaders. This change coincided with the advent of American-style conventions.

Outwardly, our party-leadership conventions and their practices do appear similar to those of our neighbours south of the border, but we have seen that such is not the case. With the extension of the U.S. primary system, Americans name their leaders long before the convention. There have been no brokered conventions in the United States since the early 1960s. Their latter-day conventions have been rather like coronations, the successful nominee known long before the fact and any excitement reserved for the approval of the party platform and the selection of the vice-presidential nominee.

Many of our political and public institutions seem to be a hybrid of British and U.S. practices. In the case of party-leadership selection practices, we have assumed the worst of both worlds. Many of the British practices are unwritten, but contemporary leadership-selection practices in Britain demand a high degree of consultation, even if these practices remain "élitist" in comparison with those of the U.S. primary system.

While British practices remain somewhat élitist, they are not corrupt. Canadian practices are both élitist and corrupt. Our democratic principles do not stand up well in comparison with U.S. practices either. Americans choose a head of state, as well as a commander-in-chief of the armed services, a head of their political party, and a head of the nation's administration. The president is all these things, yet the president's power is balanced by the power of leaders in the Congress, the Senate, and the Supreme Court. In contrast, our prime minister, although he lacks all the titles held by an American president, wields enormous power and influence in our system of parliamentary government. He names his cabinet with no recourse to legislative approval, which is required in the United States, where cabinet nominees require a two-thirds Senate vote of approval. He sets and controls the cabinet's and Parliament's agenda, and in our chaotic method of naming candidates for the House of Commons, he has an inordinate say in who can and who cannot be an official party candidate. His signature is necessary in order that a party candidate at the riding level be officially accepted and recognized. When we choose a party leader, we are often choosing a potential future prime minister who will possess vast powers — all the more reason that the choice be made in an open, democratic, and civilized way, free of corruption and élitism.

The past twenty years have seen major changes that have generally gone unnoticed by the public at large. The riding meetings that selected delegates for the conventions naming Stanfield, Trudeau, and Clark were loosely convened, informal affairs. Generally speaking, riding executives (not the membership at large) met some time before the respective conventions to see who had the time and money to go to the convention. Normally the party worker, who often had performed yeoman's service at the riding level during and between elections — the worker who would not be given time off by his or her boss — was therefore excluded. This set of circumstances also led to an unhealthy use of control and influence. A party association president with a strong bias could pack his local delegation with people who supported his choice for leader. The delegation-selection rules in force at the conventions that named Chrétien and Mulroney are there for all to see. These rules were and remain open to abuse.

As already cited, party members at the riding level had to have membership cards in order to vote for delegates for the conventions. The trouble is that there has been a very weak tradition relating to membership cards within the framework of our parties. Local riding associations closely guard their membership lists, not wanting outside interference, especially from national headquarters. That means no party really has a permanent list of card-carrying members, and there is no central control and discipline imposing uniform national standards on what constitutes a bona fide party member. In some provinces, a membership card constitutes membership in both the provincial and federal parties, a circumstance that provokes doubt about the interest of some of these members in the federal party and its processes. Surely the schoolchildren and derelicts who ripped up their membership cards after the riding meetings that selected delegates for the Tories' and Liberals' 1983 and 1984 conventions could not be considered bona fide, card-carrying party members.

Canadians will be facing an election full of issues, but the major one may well be the unpopularity of the leaders of the two leading contending parties who were chosen, without popular participation, by a corrupted and élitist system that excluded the people. Our consolation must be that people will not let these present practices continue; they will see the need for reform and act.

If we want a wider spectrum of the Canadian population to participate in selecting our leaders, we must reform the selection process, but how extensive a reform are we willing to undertake? Are we willing to examine the substance and philosophy of the process as it has existed over the past fifty years? Do we wish to dispense entirely with the convention system or simply reform it slightly? Should we reform the rules of the process of leadership selection or reform the process itself?

Reform of the Rules

For some time, I seriously considered the possibility of reforming existing convention rules, but because of latter-day tendencies to corrupt and subvert the democratic considerations behind the rules governing delegate selection, I see no hope in meaningful amendment or reformation of the convention system in Canada as we now know it. We need some system of universal suffrage, and we need reforms of our definitions of voters and of our controls on campaign contributions and spending.

Party Membership

First, it must be determined whether only party membership should vote for a party leader or whether the vote should be open to all citizens who meet the voting requirements of the

Canada Elections Act. This latter approach would leave us with a system resembling the cross-voting method used in some U.S. primaries, where Republicans can vote for Democratic candidates and vice versa. If, by contrast, we limit voting simply to bona fide members of a given political party, the definition of what constitutes a bona fide member will have to be very strict and enforceable. This method, undoubtedly, would have to involve a central national list of card-carrying party members, constituency by constituency, and there would have to be a cut-off date for selling membership cards immediately after a leadership contest is announced. We should anticipate positive and constructive debates on these issues within our various political parties as we approach the selection of future leaders.

Contributions and Spending

Running a national leadership campaign is an expensive undertaking and, with the corrupting influence of a large pool of money present, there is a need to control and account for all this campaign money to ensure that the integrity of the democratic process is restored.

Candidates who enter the race should have to name an official agent who would be responsible for all the financial aspects of the campaign. The agent should record the amounts of all contributions and their sources and should also record the nature of all disbursements. At the end of the campaign, the official agent should be responsible for turning over financial records to the national party executive for a complete and independent audit. The independent auditor would be named by the party's National Executive, and his report should be made public.

Contributions from corporations, unions, or other public or private institutions can be allowed, but these contributions should be publicly recorded. The parties should consider an upper limit for any individual contribution. A good policy might be to permit no one to contribute more than $1,000 to any given candidate. All contributions, except for those collected at fund-raising events, should be recorded, and the source identified.

One of the key problems of accountability is how to define a contribution. The definition of contribution must be limited to a cash amount, but should include all goods and services received by a candidate in the course of the campaign for the leadership. Such a definition is in accordance with the Canada Elections Act, which further demands that these contributions be recorded at the current market value. A similar accounting process for leadership campaigns should also be considered. The inclusion of services would mean that a computer consultant doing recorded work for a campaign related to his or her profession would be considered as a contributor and his or her work at its current value. However, if the same consultant were stuffing envelopes, this time would not be considered a contribution, but volunteer labour. In all cases, the official agent should issue receipts for the goods, services, and money contributed.

Eventually all contributions are turned into expenditures by the campaign organizations. Many analysts have pointed out that the spending in leadership races is out of control and will have to be reined in sooner or later. The spending limits should be fairly broad, recognizing the huge expenses that contemporary leadership campaigns require, but not so generous as to permit a candidate to buy his or her way into the leader's office by outspending his or her opponents. A good starting-point for controls would, once again, be the Canada Elections Act. The spending formulas in the act could very easily be adapted to a leadership race. The only necessary modification would be to base the allocations on the number of party members, rather than on the number of eligible voters. This solution seems the simplest to institute and enforce.

As well as recording contributions, the official agent should be charged with keeping detailed records of the disbursements made by the campaign. Spending would be defined as any outlay of money for materials or services used by the campaign or its candidate. The official agent should present all receipts and other records at the time of the final report to the auditor.

There is one other issue concerning the financial aspects of leadership races that has to be considered. In recent years, as already pointed out, some leadership candidates have exploited a loophole in the Canada Elections Act to help finance their leadership bids. The loophole permits people to contribute to the riding association of a leadership candidate. These people are then issued with a receipt granting them a tax deduction. The money collected at the riding level is then designated for use by the leadership candidate. This loophole, although legal, gives an undue advantage to MPs who are competing against non-elected opponents. To turn a problem into a solution, this loophole could be exploited to provide greater financial disclosure from leadership candidates in the future. We could make the loophole universal by insisting that all leadership-campaign contributions be channelled through the national parties. If such a system were created, a person would send a contribution to the party and indicate to which candidate the money should be directed. The party could issue a tax receipt for the contributor and a cheque, a lump sum of all contributions, to the campaign. In this way, detailed records would be kept. The amounts involved could be made public at a later date and would be open to inspection by Revenue Canada and Election Canada.

Universal Suffrage

A universal-suffrage system is potentially the simplest and most direct manner in which to select national party leaders. In theory, it widens the franchise to all party members in good standing. Each party member should be asked to cast a vote for party leader in a two-ballot voting process.

I would like to see a system of universal suffrage used to cure the ills of our present system. It is the most democratic and representative form of expressing the political will of the people, the corner-stone of our political system as it now stands. Universal suffrage would reduce the influence of party élites, corporations, and unions.

The selection of a leader by universal suffrage would involve establishing a structure similar to that used in a general election. A chief electoral officer and local returning officers would have to be named, and these officers would be responsible for holding the vote. In addition, poll clerks, ballot-boxes, and hall rentals would be required in every riding across the country. The Progressive Conservatives, NDP, and Liberals would need to establish strong grass-roots organizations if they chose to utilize a system of universal suffrage to select their leaders. An independent centralized authority would have to be created to oversee the entire process and ensure the smooth running of the campaign.

Voting should be held on a Sunday, the day it is easiest for most people to get to the polls. The balloting places should be open long enough to accommodate broad participation. In addition, there should be the possibility for advance ballots for those party members who are unable to vote at the designated time and place.

It is to be hoped that the parties would organize regional meetings where all the candidates would have a chance to air their views and to respond to questions from members. If some of these meetings were broadcast to other regions, the voting membership would have a chance to make a truly informed choice.

Voting day for party leaders should operate very much as a federal election does. People would go to their assigned voting place, where their eligibility would be verified before they were allowed to vote. The results of the voting would be tabulated for each riding and called in by telephone to party headquarters, and the totals would be made public. If no single candidate achieved a clear majority, a run-off vote between the top two finishers would be called for within a week or two.

Critics of universal suffrage complain that such a reform would be costly, and that the party or parties who would adopt such a change would lose much of the momentum, publicity, and excitement derived from the traditional conventions. I believe this is not the case. The Parti Québécois found their universal-suffrage exercise considerably cheaper than the traditional convention route. I firmly believe that would also hold true for our parties at the national level. The suspense factor would also be preserved. Imagine Election Sunday under the universal-suffrage system. Thousands of party members could be on hand from every corner of the land and from every riding in Ottawa on that day, approving party policy or an election platform. The leadership candidates would be there too. Once the winner was declared elected, he or she could address the meeting and nation on national television. At worst, if no winner was found on the first Sunday, the eventual winner would address the nation on TV on a subsequent Sunday.

Because it is based on a clear majority, universal suffrage would be less divisive for the party than the traditional convention process. In addition, it would encourage the media to pay attention to the whole race rather than to focus on the convention. Longer media exposure would increase the party's profile with the public. Moreover, the grass-roots membership would feel more involved in the process, and that in itself would be a source of greater electoral strength for a political party.

Sir Wilfrid Laurier pioneered the convention method in Canada. This method involved the politics of inclusion, relating to the rank and file of the party. It is my view that this step forward in democratizing the procedure for electing the LIberal leader played a major role in helping the Grits retain power for the greater part of this century. I believe equally firmly that the first party to adopt the universal suffrage "One Member — One Vote" method in the election of future leaders will reap similar advantages at the polls.

I have tried to paint as honest a picture of our leadership-selection process as possible. The picture that emerges shows that the Canadian method of selecting party leaders is undemocratic and unrepresentative. It is at best a smoke-and-mirrors illusion of democracy. The people see a democratic process and believe they are involved, but in reality they are pre-empted by the party élites, the large corporations and unions, and other interest groups that control the parties and make the decisions. Corporations and unions can have a place in the process, but they should not be the major decision-makers, nor should they exercise their power behind the scenes.

The blame for our situation rests less with the interest groups than with the parties themselves and the candidates who run for leadership. How can any person who believes in democracy endorse a system that encourages the busing in of children and derelicts to vote at delegate-selection meetings? How can one accept that slates of delegates are installed in the face of popular will, or that whole delegations of persons at a convention are simply named to these positions by party leaders? Universal suffrage does have drawbacks, but it seems to offer many advantages over our present system. If we want a democracy, we must, in the words of our own national anthem, stand on guard for it. Whatever system we adopt to elect our political party leaders or whatever reforms we put in place, the system will always be controlled by human beings who are fallible and corruptible. We must recognize this human limitation and ensure that the opportunities for abuse will be minimal. As democracy moves forward in Russia, old-guard élites and high Communist officials are losing their perks and limousines. In the Canadian scheme of things, if democracy is to move forward and the grass-roots to be respected, high party officials, back-room boys, and party élites will lose much of their influence, privileges, and power. That is a small price to pay.

PART THREE

WHO CONTROLS THE PURSE STRINGS?

9

TAXATION WITHOUT REPRESENTATION

The present government is in deep trouble over the Goods and Services Tax (GST). The trouble stems not so much from the nature of the tax, as from how its provisions were prepared by the Finance department. Like budgets, this major tax legislation was prepared in total secrecy by Finance officials. While Don Blenkarn, the chairman of the Commons Finance Committee, did yeoman's service in bringing the GST out of the closet for public debate, much damage had already been done to the government. Why? The answer lies largely in the fact that the GST provisions were prepared with the same strict secrecy that surrounds budget-making. Elected representatives of the people and cabinet ministers normally are consulted and have some input into government legislation. The powerful Finance department is immune from this general rule. Budgets and the GST have been finalized by officials and announced by the Finance department without public debate or consultation, and without reference to cabinet or the government's parliamentary caucus. By any standard, democracy suffers as the people's representatives lose control of the purse strings.

After I was sworn in as minister of state for Social Programmes and Science and Technology in 1979, it didn't take long for me to realize that the Finance department wielded unlimited power. Much to my surprise and, at times, indignation, Finance officials sat in on cabinet meetings and even attended cabinet committee meetings representing the minister and speaking on his behalf. It became all too clear to me that the Finance department enjoyed privileges denied other ministries. What is worse, it enjoyed immunity from cabinet scrutiny and public and caucus debate — immunity denied other ministers and their departments. How could such fundamental rules of democracy be broken? We must look back.

Towards the end of 1959 and at the beginning of 1960, it became apparent that the Department of Finance could get the government into a lot of trouble. Little did I know how true this would be for Diefenbaker and the successive governments of Pearson, Trudeau, Clark, Trudeau again, and Mulroney. Even before Diefenbaker, in the last budget before the Grits lost power, Walter Harris, St. Laurent's Finance minister, hurt the Liberal cause with his six-dollar pension hike. By the beginning of 1986, Michael Wilson had been stung by his statements on the universality of social programs, the government's role in the collapse of two banks in western Canada, and the provision in his first budget to de-index old-age pensions. When the Finance department and its ministers can do so much damage, surely we must ask some basic questions and propose solutions. Responsible ministers cannot merely blame the system when a political storm blows up because budgets drawn up in secrecy have not been checked out by the elected representatives of the people.

"No taxation without representation" constituted a central theme of the people's claims as parliamentary democracy evolved in Britain. The same cry was heard in the American colonies in the 1770s. To be taxed only by duly elected representatives soon became the hallmark of most of the legislative institutions in the free world.

How ironic it is that a few hundred years later, successive auditors general have informed Parliament and the Canadian people that our legislators have lost their ability to control the purse strings effectively. Harold Laski, in his 1938 work *Parliamentary Government in England*, stated: "Finance is not something apart from policy but an expression of it. By deciding what to do in other spheres, the House largely decides by inference what it is to do in the financial sphere." In Canada today, budgets far surpass throne speeches in their importance. Few, if any, government initiatives escape the influence of the Department of Finance, which is a central department of state. The most important means by which Parliament rose to its historic position of supremacy was the power over the purse.

The principle that the redress of grievances must precede supply — the voting of monies by Parliament — was developed under the Normans. The Stamp Act of March 1765 made trouble for Westminster in Britain's North American colonies, but it was soon to be followed by the Quartering Act. The British intended to enforce taxation without representation in the American colonies. Americans had to buy stamps of various kinds, ranging in price from a few pence to several pounds, to be placed on different classes of legal documents and newspapers. The British could not have imposed a more unpopular measure on the American colonists. H. C. Allen in his book *A Concise History of the USA* wrote: "Deeds and mortgages relating to property, licenses to practice law, licenses to sell liquor, college diplomas, playing cards, dice, almanacs, and calendars all had to bear British stamps of stated values. More than this: publishers and printers of advertisements, newspapers, and other sheets had to buy stamps for their publications. If the British Parliament had deliberately searched for taxes that would annoy as many Americans as possible, it could scarcely have improved upon the Stamp Act."

Lawyers and merchants were quick to voice their resentment against it. The cry "No taxation without representation" was taken up in cities, towns, and the countryside by artisans, mechanics, farmers, and housewives. Popular societies, called the Sons of Liberty and the Daughters of Liberty, were organized to resist the sale of stamps. Crowds gathered in the streets of Boston, New York, Philadelphia, and Charleston and rioted against officers who tried to force people to buy the stamps. The offices and houses of royal officials were stoned and in some cases sacked and burned. Going far beyond blocking the sale of stamps, Americans organized groups to boycott British goods. There was so much disorder in several colonies that even the protesting merchants and lawyers became frightened and tried to restrain the torrent of popular anger. Eventually, in 1766, the Stamp Act was repealed, as control of the purse strings and taxation, by the people in the colonies, was paramount.

One of the notions that has weakened our present-day Parliament's control over the nation's purse strings is the continued belief in budgetary secrecy. In the United States, many budgetary provisions have been given advance publicity so that public debate can take place. Although no one should be able to gain financially from being privy to advance information about budgetary intentions, there is still no excuse for the crippling secrecy that surrounds budget-making within the Canadian Parliament. Mitchell Sharp came to this conclusion after serving as Lester Pearson's Finance minister and told me as much in conversation.

It is arguable that the devaluation of the Canadian dollar during the 1962 election cost the Diefenbaker government many seats. It was done in the middle of the campaign, without full cabinet approval or parliamentary debate. In December 1982, during a meeting at York University, I asked Bob Bryce, formerly a deputy minister of Finance and clerk of the Privy Council, why devaluation and budgetary measures were prepared in such secrecy. Bryce cited the danger of advance leaks and the disconcerting effects that these might have in international markets. Little was said of the fact that over the centuries, the power of the purse had passed from the hands of despotic kings into the bowels of an unresponsive bureaucracy. You can cut kings' heads off, but bureaucracies are hard to personalize; individual public servants are more often than not civilized and decent people.

Bryce went on to say that by and large, budget considerations and proposals were very complex, so that it was often hard to explain them clearly to cabinet ministers and members of Parliament. The business executives in attendance reacted with consternation, knowing what would happen in the private sector if senior officials of a company could not give clear and understandable explanations of policy direction.

Canada is not alone in its inordinate preoccupation with budget secrecy. The Dalton case in Britain's post-war Labour government is a classic example. A supplementary budget was to be introduced at Westminster because of mounting financial difficulties in the country. On his way to the House of Commons, Hugh Dalton, the chancellor of the exchequer, passed a correspondent in the lobby, and they briefly discussed some aspects of the proposed budget. Parts of the budget appeared in *The Star* before they were presented to the House. Minutes before Dalton began reading his budget speech, *The Star* came out with headlines reading "Penny on Beer, Tax on Pools and Dogs Likely." Dalton had been a loyal member of the wartime cabinet, and Churchill was very conciliatory as leader of the opposition, not pressing for an immediate resignation. However, Churchill asked that a select committee investigate the affair. The next morning, Clement Attlee and other cabinet colleagues tried to dissuade Dalton from resigning, but after Churchill's demand for a select committee became known, Dalton tendered his resignation and it was accepted.

By the time I was appointed parliamentary secretary to the minister of Finance, George Nowlan, in the late summer of 1962, the Diefenbaker government had already been rocked by successive clashes with the governor of the Bank of Canada, James Coyne, and by the necessity to devalue the dollar during the recent election campaign. Donald Fleming, the former minister of Finance, liked nothing better than partisan confrontation, and Finance officials were only too glad to supply him with ammunition.

I soon discovered how immune the Finance department was from traditional political debate and discipline. Walter Gordon's first budget was rushed in and put before the House without serious consideration. Under a haze of nationalistic provisions to Canadianize much of the country's industries, Gordon divided the cabinet, and his budget was left in a shambles. He eventually had to resign.

Then there was Allan MacEachen's famous budgetary thrust in 1981, so out of tune with the times that the vast majority of its provisions were soon withdrawn or forgotten. Some of its specific provisions could have crippled the Canadian life-insurance industry. His credibility shattered, MacEachen was almost immediately removed to the more exotic climes of External Affairs. Who will ever forget John Crosbie's plans to tax at the pumps, an effort that handed the opposition an unexpected weapon! This move by my colourful ex-colleague from Newfoundland constituted an act of masochism that prompted more pain than gain for the Clark government, leading to its immediate downfall on prime-time television before an incredulous nation. There was also Bob Stanfield's conversion to fiscal statesmanship by officials of the Bank of Canada after the Grits had been defeated on the money bill in the House just before the 1968 Liberal leadership convention. Officials in Finance and from the Bank of Canada convinced Stanfield that to defeat the budget measures in question would do irreparable harm to Canada, and he ordered an end to the Tory filibuster.

A number of events involving the Department of Finance, all of which had serious political repercussions, took place during Diefenbaker's second Parliament. Don Fleming was a formidable opposition member, hard working, well briefed, and ready to do political battle at the drop of a hat. Political confrontation was his forte, as he had shown when he led the Tory troops during the famous pipeline debate. As Finance minister, he had an instinct for going for the political jugular that soon became apparent in the House when perhaps a little diplomacy and soft talk would have expedited his measures more easily through Parliament. Doug Abbott, St. Laurent's able Finance minister, often charmed the House, and his sense of humour invariably saved the day for him and the government when difficult and contentious issues were before the Commons. Not so Fleming. His first major confrontation took place early in the 1958 Parliament, and the lesson to be learned from it was that you should never take on a provincial premier unless your political ground is secure; the premier is normally closer to the voters. The issue was Canada, Newfoundland, and Term 29; it concerned Ottawa's obligations to the country's newest province. The disagreement over Term 29 caused half the Conservatives in the Newfoundland Assembly to bolt the party and form one of their own. It also gave rise to a snap election that showed Canada that Newfoundland felt the federal government had failed to live up to its obligations. Smallwood gained a resounding victory at the polls.

Representatives of Newfoundland were at Québec in 1864, but although provisions had been made in the British North America Act of 1867 for Newfoundland to enter

Canada, union was rejected decisively in the 1869 Newfoundland election. In 1895, Newfoundland again considered the possibility of joining Canada, but the financial problems proved insoluble, and negotiations foundered. In 1946, a Confederation movement again got under way, and the next year a delegation arrived in Ottawa to "ascertain federal union." In agreeing to meet the delegation, the King government pointed out the need to have a complete and comprehensive exchange of information between the governments of Newfoundland and Canada. Canada's view of the need for careful consideration led to the formation of ten subcommittees. Joey Smallwood was a member of each!

After the deliberations, Ottawa considered the suggestions and adopted a basis for union that was sent to Newfoundland. In the accompanying letter, King carefully pointed out that "as far as the financial aspects of the proposed arrangements for union are concerned, the government of Canada believes that the arrangements go as far as the government can go under the circumstances." Term 14 in the document, setting forth the proposed basis of union, referred to a royal commission to recommend additional financial assistance for Newfoundland, if it was needed.

The terms of union were approved and assented to by the Newfoundland legislature on Friday 18, 1949. Term 29 read as follows:

> In view of the difficulty of predicting with sufficient accuracy the financial consequences to Newfoundland of becoming a province of Canada, the government of Canada will appoint a Royal Commission within eight years from the date of union to review the financial position of the Province of Newfoundland and to recommend the form and scale of additional financial assistance, if any, that may be required to continue

public services at the levels and standards reached subsequent to the date of Union, without resorting to taxation more burdensome, having regard to capacity to pay, than that obtaining generally in the region comprising the Maritime provinces of Nova Scotia, New Brunswick and Prince Edward Island.

Up to 1962, Ottawa had contributed $8 million to the Newfoundland government. The catch was the preamble to the federal bill covering financial assistance to the province. It stated that the situation would merely be reviewed in 1962, and disregarded the notion of payments in perpetuity. The political fallout was predictable: Smallwood hammered away at Ottawa's stinginess. I suspected that the federal Department of Finance and its officials were sometimes isolated from the customary political debate between Ottawa and St. John's. Few diplomatic or political skills were employed. That is not to say that Smallwood was Simon Pure, or easy to deal with, but even in our own caucus, a number of Newfoundland members and their families had voted against Confederation. Indeed, on the day following the vote for Confederation, many Newfoundlanders had draped their homes in black. The Term 29 debate was full of political danger for Ottawa and eventually hurt the Diefenbaker government. The Finance department, with its immunity from political control, played its part in the debate.

Economic issues continued to haunt Diefenbaker right up to the next election. As the 1962 campaign came to an end, Diefenbaker drove from Ottawa to the West Island of Montréal for a luncheon meeting, where he would support the candidacy of the sitting member, Marcel Bourbonnais. Afterwards, the prime minister invited me to join him and his wife on the drive to my riding, where he was to speak on my behalf at the Cowansville town hall. As usual with Dief, the conversation en route was animated. The prime minister ate one candy after another, and when we arrived at our destination, the floor of the car was covered with discarded wrappers. He was pessimistic about the outcome of the election, so much so that he suggested that we would not even be able to form a minority government. His pessimism was well founded. Diefenbaker told me that he had canvassed the cabinet before he saw the Governor General, in order to determine whether any troublesome issues were in the wind. On May 2, in the middle of the campaign, Donald Fleming had announced that the government had fixed the foreign exchange rate of the Canadian dollar at 92.5 cents against the American dollar. The issue gained incredible political momentum and was soon termed the "devaluation" of the Canadian dollar. When he canvassed his cabinet on the advisability of calling an election, Diefenbaker claimed that nothing had ever been mentioned about the pegging of the dollar by his Finance minister or, alternatively, by any officials from Finance or the Bank of Canada.

On the outskirts of Cowansville, we were met by a marching band that led us into the town hall. A young teenager on a ten-speed bicycle approached our car to get a good look at the prime minister. To do this, the young boy had thrown his bike out of gear, and he had to pedal madly to keep his balance. The bicycle remained almost stationary as the frenzied pedalling took place. Dief peered out of the car, watching the forward pedalling that was creating no advance motion, and quipped, "He's going nowhere, just like our campaign."

It was the first time since 1950 that the government had undertaken to maintain the value of our dollar at a fixed rate. The move came less than a month after Fleming had explained in his budget speech why it was inappropriate for Canada to fix the exchange rate, as it had been urged to do for almost a year by the International Monetary Fund.

Opposition spokesmen said that devaluation would immediately increase the cost of living because the price of imported goods would shoot up. Our large balance-of-payments deficit was there for all to see; Canadians were living well beyond their means.

In April, there had been a drop of $115 million in government holdings. This was the sixth decline in a row, and, since October, the treasury had poured $516 million of its American-dollar holdings into the exchange market in order to prevent the value of the Canadian dollar from dropping below the ninety-five-cent level. Large capital imports over a long period were, in part, responsible for the situation.

The opposition's broadsides began immediately. Walter Gordon said, "This is an awful time to do a thing like this. Mr. Fleming would not have done it unless the situation was out of control." He went on to say that the news would add to international nervousness about Canadian fiscal policies.

The floating-rate-of-exchange policy was over. The timing of the decision and the rate adopted seemed to have been imposed on the government by external forces. The post-war honeymoon was coming to an end. As our trading partners became more self-reliant, they had less need for our goods and services.

Soon after Fleming's announcement, the Liberal opposition flooded the country with Diefendollars. These were copies of the Canadian dollar, but with a portion cut off at the end, dramatically demonstrating the effects of the devaluation. The press soon took up the slogan.

Over 80 per cent of Canada's population lives within two hundred miles of the American border. The political implications of devaluation were immeasurable, especially in ridings along the border, and the rising political rhetoric deeply wounded the government, which went on to lose a record number of seats — nearly a hundred. I believe that

Diefenbaker's gutsy performance on the hustings saved the government from a rout and allowed it to continue in a majority situation after the election. It is incredible to think Fleming decided to devalue in the middle of a campaign, without the matter being discussed by the full cabinet and caucus. Yet this indicates how immune from the real world were the Finance mandarins.

After the election, Diefenbaker was in low spirits. I visited him at 24 Sussex Drive early on an August morning, and some days later he asked me to become the parliamentary secretary to the minister of Finance. At the time of my visit, Dief was walking with a cane. A few days before, he had broken a small bone in his ankle as he stumbled on a flagstone path outside his house at Harrington Lake. The deputy minister, Ken Taylor, took great pains to introduce me to the department's senior staff. George Nowlan, my minister, was a wonderful colleague. He knew how to delegate and had proved to be a strong and effective minister of National Revenue. Like Doug Abbott's before him, his charm and candour in the House helped him over many troubles, and he had excellent political instincts. Had our government lasted a little longer, I am convinced that he would have been a first-class minister of Finance. As it was, our budget never saw the light of day.

One of my principal tasks, being a bilingual Quebecker, was to advise Nowlan on the political implications of the Créditistes and their leader, Réal Caouette, who had hurt us and the Liberals in the province. Caouette's appeal was potent and devastating. It was directed to low- and middle-income families who had been hit by higher interest rates and the credit squeeze. His arguments had been ignored by the Conservatives. Such continued to be the case as we started our minority mandate. The Finance department could not be counted on to have much insight into or sensitivity for the issue. In 1962, there were few, if any, officials at the department who spoke French or understood Québec's aspirations. In October, I was responsible for piloting a finance bill through the House committee stage. On such occasions, since highly technical questions have to be answered, a senior official usually sits with documentation at a table in the aisle of the chamber, right in front of the minister or parliamentary secretary. The official listens intently to opposition remarks and whispers advice to the government spokesman. On this occasion, Caouette had gone on for quite a while, articulating social-credit theory with his usual humour and gusto. He had made a number of points that I could have handled in a general political way, but there were obviously some technical facts, or perhaps non-facts, to be dealt with.

The able assistant deputy minister remained silent during Caouette's harangue. When the Créditiste leader had finally finished, I leaned forward and asked the official if he had any facts for me before I replied. He smiled and said, "I am only here to advise you on things of this world."

Officials in Finance and at the Bank of Canada are totally isolated from and immune from the political effects of their decisions, especially when it comes to interest rates and matters such as "taxing at the pumps" and the GST. It all comes down to this. When ancient kings taxed, there was taxation without representation. Control of the purse strings by "the people" constituted a fundamental freedom in the emergence of parliamentary democracies. Today, in Canada, the bureaucracy largely controls the purse strings, using Parliament as a rubber stamp. That has been most evident in the debate over the GST. We have abdicated one of our fundamental freedoms — no longer do we truly have "taxation with representation."

10

DISASTROUS BUDGETS AND DEFEATED GOVERNMENTS

Between 1963 and 1984 the federal Department of Finance, which normally is distanced from political realities, was at the centre of three disastrous budgets and the defeat of the government on a money bill. Before the 1963 election, Walter Gordon repeated time and again that a new Liberal administration would usher in a legislative program that he called "sixty days of decision." The "sixty days" slogan was a phrase borrowed from John Kennedy's first weeks of office in the United States (sixty days of action referred to the period just after Kennedy's election). Gordon's proposals were hastily prepared and ill conceived.

Heading this series of blunders was Gordon's first budget, presented on June 13, 1963. Officials of the department of Finance could not be blamed for it. Gordon's relations with his deputy minister, Kenneth Taylor, were cool, to say the least. The minister had called upon outside advisers, mostly from Toronto, to help him prepare his budget. The fact that he had relied on outside advice was revealed only after persistent questioning in the House by Doug Fisher, the NDP member for Port Arthur. Officials at the Department of Finance were so annoyed that many of them seemed indifferent about whether the minister survived. As Gordon was valiantly attempting to pilot some of his budgetary provisions through the House, my colleague George Nowlan called me over in the Commons chamber and pointed out that none of our old friends from the Finance department were in the officials' gallery. This gallery is normally reserved for senior public servants who wish to attend debates when matters affecting their ministry are being discussed. Senior mandarins can quickly pass advice down to their minister and be immediately in touch with general proceedings and developments. Irked at Gordon's decision to hire outside consultants, most senior Finance officials boycotted his budget speech and the subsequent debate. The carpet was being gently pulled out from under the feet of a new and idealistic minister.

As a nationalist, Walter Gordon advocated measures that he felt would encourage the indigenous economic growth and ownership of Canada's economy. He met strong opposition within the cabinet, especially from Mitchell Sharp. Furthermore, his own deputy minister, Ken Taylor, had no sympathy for Gordon's views, since Canada had to attract foreign capital, especially from the United States. Eric Kierans, a fellow Liberal, publicly called Gordon's budget foolish and unrealistic. The budget was in a shambles. Even if many of Gordon's economic goals were laudable, his hurriedly cobbled-together proposals were not feasible or attractive to voters. Yet what contributed most to his downfall was the absence of political control over budget-making.

Eventually most of Gordon's proposals were withdrawn or modified. He had fallen at the starting gate, never to recover, his reputation and party standing in tatters. While he did not immediately resign, this initial disaster was a prime factor in his eventual departure from the Finance portfolio. Most influential Liberals saw him as an impetuous maverick.

Budgets can bring down more than ministers. The headlines in many papers across the land on February 20, 1968, read "Liberals beaten 84-82." Mike Pearson, who had announced that he would be stepping down as leader and prime minister, was in Jamaica, and his party was in the throes of a leadership race. On the night of a Commons vote, the deputy prime minister, Paul Martin, and two Liberal backbenchers were in Trois-Rivières for a leadership campaign meeting. After the defeat of the government bill to raise taxes by imposing a 5 per cent surcharge on personal income tax, Bob Stanfield called on the government to resign. Tommy Douglas said that if the government tried to restore its position in the Commons by asking for a vote of confidence, his party would oppose it. The whole procedural fiasco was a terrible embarrassment for Mitchell Sharp, who had leadership aspirations of his own. It was he who had presented the government's bill.

Robert Winters, the Trade minister and the number-three man in the cabinet pecking order, quickly summoned an emergency meeting of senior ministers. He, too, had leadership hopes and wished to minimize the damage to himself as the man in charge. Such learned fellows as Eugene Forsey offered convoluted constitutional explanations to suggest that the minority government could carry on despite the fact that it had been defeated on a money bill. Pearson hurried back from the Caribbean, but it was clear that the cabinet was deeply divided on the best course of action to take.

On February 21, Pearson was lustily cheering at his party caucus. We held our own caucus at the same time and claimed that the government had no right to stay in office. Stanfield decided that the Conservatives would boycott committee meetings. Pearson faced an angry opposition and challenged it by presenting a tough confidence motion. Yet the motion was not all that simple or straightforward.

Pearson asked the Commons to vote that its defeat of the government's tax increases did not constitute non-confidence in the government. The debate was slated to start on the following Friday, and I began to sense a slight softening in the opposition's stance. Although I have never thought that we should blindly follow British constitutional precedent, I could not help thinking of Westminster during this parliamentary turmoil. It is unlikely that such an amateurish mistake would have happened there, but if it had, the government probably would have been more contrite and the opposition more bullish. Yet in Britain they never keep one party in power for very long, and no single party gets infected with the "divine right to rule" disease.

I thought that there were several political risks in precipitating an election during the Liberals' leadership race, but did not entirely appreciate the advice that Stanfield was given by Finance department officials, who told him that the defeat of the tax measures would do incalculable damage to Canada at home and abroad. Their advice made Stanfield more cautious, and he said that he would not allow a filibuster during the Commons debate. I often wondered if the decent and statesmanlike Stanfield realized that he was being counselled by many of the same advisers who had said that we must devalue during the 1962 election campaign.

Réal Caouette declared he would oppose the government, but, in a few days he had changed his mind, saying that he had lost faith in both the NDP and Conservatives. That fired up Diefenbaker, and in the debate that followed, he implied that the Créditiste *volte face* was a scandal, and resurrected stories that financier John Doyle had influenced the Créditistes to support the new Pearson government in 1963. Gordon Churchill quit the Tory caucus to sit as an Independent Conservative because the party was caving in. Earlier in the week, our caucus had agreed to allow the government motion to come to a vote without a filibuster. That meant that the government was off the hook and that the 84–82 vote against its crucial tax bill was not a vote of nonconfidence. Churchill felt basic principles were being violated, and he had many allies on our back benches.

The vote took place on February 28. Only one Tory, who had been ill, failed to appear, and the Liberals won by 138 to 119. The government was saved. Perhaps because the Grits were waging a leadership race, political considerations dictated that sooner or later the government would be let off the hook, but once more, budget secrecy and the Finance department's immunity from the usual imperatives of political life contributed to the crisis and, more important, to its ultimate resolution.

Only after sixteen years in opposition did we finally get our chance again. I had the honour to serve in government with some excellent cabinet colleagues; with time, I thought that we would become an effective administration. Soon after I was sworn in to the cabinet as minister of Science and Technology I came to realize that while ministers must master their own portfolios, they court disaster if they do not understand the workings and powers of the Prime Minister's Office, the Privy Council Office, the Treasury Board, and the Department of Finance. While the prime minister, then Joe Clark, would have been the first to accept the blame for our defeat in the House and ultimately at the polls, once more the political immunity, and consequent stupidity, of the Finance department largely contributed to our downfall.

Cabinet documents are normally supplied to ministers before meetings of the full cabinet or its committees so they can assess the political implications of decisions that may be taken in the full cabinet. The only minister who escapes these procedural requirements is the Finance minister. He,

DISASTROUS BUDGETS

his deputy, and the prime minister, and sometimes the clerk of the Privy Council, are really the only people who are fully briefed on the import of the budget before its final form is put before the House. This tradition has exacted an unnecessary political toll and will continue to do so until the whole question of the budget's preparation is reformed. Budgets usually have grave political implications. The fact that they are formulated with no proper political vetting seems incredible. No amount of prior consultation with interested parties can begin to replace parliamentary control over budget-making. No Canadian minister of Finance consulted more broadly than Michael Wilson. However, that did not prevent him from plunging into trouble with his first budget.

John Crosbie's budget of December 11, 1979, might seem in retrospect quite a statesmanlike document, but for a minority government just getting under way, it was political Russian roulette and bravado heavily sprinkled with a good dose of subliminal Tory masochism. The proposed changes would affect the capital-gains tax and help farmers and small businessmen, but nobody on the opposition benches noticed that or talked about it. An immediate excise tax on gasoline was what did it; it's all I heard about in every corner of my riding during the ensuing election campaign. The fact that the Liberals subsequently compounded the felony does not seem to matter. The Conservatives were about to lose power. When we finally went down on prime-time television, I made no apologies for having lost my cool in public during an interview on the French-language network in the lobby of the Commons, after the vote.

Few people can claim the title "a House of Commons man." Stanley Knowles and John Diefenbaker are two who could. To obtain such recognition requires an intuitive sense of the House and its peculiar moods. Allan MacEachen was also a superb parliamentarian who knew how to parry and thrust when the going got rough, with his uncanny debating style and knowledge of the rules of the House. He almost single-handedly engineered the collapse of the Clark government in December 1979. It is hard to imagine a man with such astute political instincts becoming entrapped in the labyrinths of the Finance department. Yet that was the case when he presented his second budget on November 12, 1981.

Admittedly, it was not entirely the fault of the senior mandarins in Finance. At a time when the economy was in the doldrums and when the private sector needed stimulus, MacEachen presented an astonishing budget. The minister's left-of-centre views, instilled during his days at St. Francis Xavier University, the spiritual home of the Co-operative Movement, were just not suited to the times. Officials at Finance worked overtime, poring over the flow charts. It seems that they were preparing a budget for another country, at another time, and in another world. Provisions to help farmers, developers, and small business just would not fly. Deferred annuities were to be hit hard. If enacted, these provisions would have seriously crippled Canada's insurance industry, as noted; subsequently, they were to be largely and conveniently ignored.

The Canadian Tax Act is unnecessarily complex compared with those in other Western democracies, and MacEachen's blunderbuss attempt at tax reform proved to be a disaster. During my years on the Hill, no budget suffered more from public opprobrium than MacEachen's second effort. Most of its central proposals were withdrawn or ignored; the minister's reputation as a superb political tactician was left in shreds.

Conventional wisdom has it that those who accept the Finance portfolio are digging their own political graves. If that is true, it is not because the minister often has to initiate unpopular measures. For the most part, the public would understand that. It is because the minister invariably has to do so within the framework of outdated procedures, cloaked in secrecy, that he is denied the capacity to take the necessary soundings of the House and the country. How else did such stalwarts as Fleming, Gordon, Crosbie, and MacEachen bite the political dust?

In April 1982, MacEachen issued "A Paper on Budget Secrecy and Proposals for Broader Consultation" to try to allay public criticism. Leaders of labour and industry in the private sector and politicians and government officials in other departments affected by Finance's extensive power cried out for immediate reform. MacEachen had to move. I can do no better than cite the preface to his paper: "In reply to a question in the House of Commons on December 10, 1981, I said: 'It may be that the House of Commons ought to consider, at some time, revising the attitude towards budget secrecy to make it possible to have a more meaningful consultation prior to the budget presentation.'"

MacEachen's paper was intended to stimulate the public discussion necessary to modify the tradition of budget secrecy. Some background observations make interesting reading. Ministers in the past had much to say. Walter Gordon observed: "The old established tradition — according to which budgets are prepared in the Department of Finance, without consultation or discussion with other officials or outside experts, and without informing the cabinet of what is going to be proposed hours before presentation to the House — should be changed."

In 1969, Edgar Benson, a minister of Finance, stated: "What I would like is for the minister to be able to present a tentative basis of his proposal to Parliament for discussion. The way it is now, the minister of Finance has to present highly important advice from a very small group of expert advisers in a form which the government can understand, and on this the government stands or falls, and I think this is wrong."

Donald Macdonald, in his budget speech of May 1976, said: "The time has come to consider whether some of the long-standing traditions that surround the budgetary process should be modified to serve better the needs of today." He added: "Two aspects of the budgetary process require particular study. The first is the strict rule of secrecy that applies to the budget prior to its introduction. The second is the procedure for consideration of the budget proposals following their introduction in Parliament."

The Honourable John Crosbie stated in 1979: "I hope it will be possible in the coming session of Parliament to examine the entire process of budget-making. We could begin by referring the entire area to a committee of the House of Commons."

MacEachen's paper underlined the necessity for creating a more open pre-budget process: "The original concept of budget secrecy was thus relatively narrow: To protect against financial advantage or gain." However, he went on, "the tradition inhibits consultations within the government. The recent introduction of the government's expenditure management system has greatly expanded the need for extensive interdepartmental and interministerial discussions in the pre-budget period." Moreover, "the extreme interpretation of budget secrecy does not take account of the broad economic and social role which modern budgets must play." MacEachen concluded that "a redefinition of budget secrecy thus is necessary to ensure that broader consultation and a more meaningful response to pre-budget submissions from the public is possible."

The paper suggested that consultative bodies be established, and that a permanent advisory committee be set up, consisting of outside tax specialists, to provide advice on a regular basis to the minister of Finance and his officials. The Canadian Tax Foundation recommended that a tax-reform commission be established as a permanent body, which would be independent of the government and Parliament. MacEachen's paper also noted:

> The redefinition of budget secrecy would contribute to an improved framework within which public consultations in the pre-budget period could take place. Other positive steps would be for a minister of Finance to issue green papers, white papers, or other less formal documents providing information on certain policy or technical issues that he wanted to address in a future budget. This would inform those with a particular interest or expertise that an area of tax policy was under consideration and enable them to make representations before final decisions are taken. The release of background papers on certain policy initiatives or technical changes that are under consideration also would undoubtedly serve to improve the two-way communication process. This is particularly so in those complex areas of the law where the government cannot be expected to have all the information necessary for a full assessment of the impact of proposed changes.

MacEachen recommended the idea of a regular date to present the budget each year; such scheduling would overcome the uncertainties that now exist and would allow for an organized preparation of the budget. A fall date was suggested.

We should never forget that the budget is a political document and that therefore changes must take place in the House of Commons itself. The executive should retain decision-making authority, but members of Parliament themselves should define and determine the political climate.

Past studies of the budget process have underlined two basic problems: (a) there is insufficient opportunity for the broadest possible debate on major initiatives of taxation policy; and (b) there is insufficient opportunity to correct technical deficiencies in tax legislation.

Many people have recommended that the secrecy rule be amended to obviate the disclosure of information that if known might provide private advantage. The one recommendation that must be acted on immediately is that all taxation bills in draft form should be submitted to a standing committee of the House of Commons for clause-by-clause scrutiny.

What most governments lack is a feeling of the mood of the country, which Parliament normally accords to the legislative process. As James Burns and Timothy Denton wrote in a paper on the budget process: "The practice initiated in the June 28, 1982, budget of referring complex proposals to outside experts after another budget for technical analysis is an excellent one. These individuals are not asked — nor would their training and non-political backgrounds compel them — to comment on the political philosophy or advisability of a proposal. Their task is to translate a government's stated policy objectives into legislation and regulations which will most effectively achieve what is desired."

This is an important consideration. Many ex-ministers have told me they would never have presented certain legislation to the House if they had realized how much subsequent regulations and interpretation would ruin their original intentions for the principle of the legislation.

In my view, the pre-budget debate should be focused in public hearings before a special committee of Parliament, and the Department of Finance's forecast of the economy in the coming year should be the basic document — the *raison d'être* of the debate.

Undoubtedly, the Department of Finance must be the dominant economic portfolio. I well remember the constructive role its officials played when, as minister of Science and

Technology, I weighed the pros and cons of increased tax incentives for industrial research and development. On the one hand, it is imperative that we get the debate about the budget process out of the rut of secrecy in which it is now mired. A better budgetary process is one precondition for restoring to Parliament its traditional rights of proper control over the purse strings. The rewards for the country will be incalculable. Surely recent events should have converted Michael Wilson to the cause. His GST is a case in point. These tax proposals, whether good or bad, were never vetted by the full cabinet; nor did they receive proper scrutiny by the government caucus. Drafted in secrecy by the bureaucracy, with no public dialogue or input, they were announced to a public totally unaware of the principles behind the tax. Now the government is faced with the impossible task of explaining the GST in the face of a political storm. Once more, unnecessary damage has been done to a government already in deep trouble.

Part Four

Bureaucratic Control

11

Majority Government 1958

Comparing the events and circumstances surrounding March 31, 1958, when John Diefenbaker and his Progressive Conservative government came to power, with Mulroney's victory of September 4, 1984, and arriving at hasty conclusions, could be hazardous. Yet there are some striking parallels. Perhaps Brian Mulroney does not share John Diefenbaker's paranoia about the top ranks of the permanent public service, but Diefenbaker had reason for scepticism. When Mike Pearson took over as prime minister on April 9, 1963, one of the first things he did was to convene a meeting with all deputy ministers. It was like old-home week. By and large, the senior bureaucrats collectively breathed a sign of relief as Diefenbaker made his exit and their old colleague again took the helm. They greeted Pearson with open arms, believing that things would return to normal once more after the Tory interregnum.

What other country that took government seriously would tolerate what happened next? Pearson named several former deputy ministers and other senior public servants to his cabinet. Sitting across from me on the treasury benches were Pearson himself, who had been under-secretary of state for External Affairs; Bud Drury, the former deputy minister of

National Defence; Mitchell Sharp, ex–deputy minister of Trade and Commerce; and Jack Pickersgill, who had been clerk of the Privy Council under Mackenzie King and St. Laurent. On the government side, we often referred to Jack as "The Pick." He claimed more than once that Diefenbaker and the Tories were overly paranoid about the public service. Yet he did nothing himself to allay our suspicions. While in opposition, he continually sought advice on broadcast policy from Alphonse Ouimet, then president of the Canadian Broadcasting Corporation. Next we had Pierre Juneau, who ran unsuccessfully for the Grits in Hochelaga, heading the CBC. Back in power as Transport minister, Pickersgill piloted legislation through the Commons to set up the Canadian Transport Commission. Once the bill was passed, he resigned from politics, but not before being named the first chairman of the new Transport Commission. Not bad if you can get away with it! And Jack did.

Once in a while, there is no doubt that a civil servant should move into the partisan political arena, but what took place in 1963 was a disgrace. It was bad for Canada because politicized public servants usually tell their political masters what they want to hear, not necessarily what they should hear.

Although Trudeau did not adorn his cabinet benches with former civil servants, he did something even worse. He appointed his crony Michael Pitfield to be clerk of the Privy Council; in short order they set out, with no little success, to politicize one of the best civil services in the world. A lot of harm was done. Pitfield played the innocent, pretending that he had never been a true Grit. Trudeau's protégé, Michael Kirby, created almost as much havoc as Pitfield in the senior ranks of the public service, where political subservience was preferred to objective advice based on what was best for the country. Now, like the former, he has gone to his reward in the Senate, if that's still considered a reward these days.

Before September 4, 1984, with an interlude of only a little over six years, one Canadian political party had been in power for more than forty years. Mulroney inherited a tough situation with the federal public service. That is not to say that its senior echelons are inhabited solely by Liberals, nor that the vast majority of them are not loyal and competent. But it is to say that, effectively, they had only one master for well over three decades. Mulroney's administration had no greater challenge than to get a lever on policy-making and to ensure that the public service carried out the government's will. Diefenbaker's inability to meet this challenge was decisive in the downfall of his administration.

Of course, the public service must help formulate policy, but it should not have the exclusive right to do so. Policy decisions submitted to me as a minister rarely gave me valid options; I mainly was presented with the bureaucracy's one-sided bias. In Washington, cabinet officers are normally briefed by White House staff and by officials of their respective departments; the presidential system presents them with feasible choices and viable alternatives. By and large, senior public officials in Canada are averse to seeking ideas from the private sector, as they jealously protect their right to give policy advice to "the minister."

After being sworn in as a member of Parliament, I got to work as the "ombudsman" — the "spokesman" — for Brome-Missisquoi in the House of Commons. Helping constituents solve problems with their pensions, family allowances, and unemployment-insurance cheques; working to bring new industry into the riding; speaking out on national issues in caucus and in the House were but a few of the duties that made the job fulfilling for me.

Members often work on Parliament Hill from early morning to late at night. They beat a track there from their home, apartment, or hotel room, and rarely have time to get to know the city or its environs. For one day and one night, my family stayed with me in Ottawa, and after they left, I grew quite lonely. But at least I was young and single.

Arthur Miller's classic play *Death of a Salesman* portrays the tragic dilemma of a man who has so refined his skills and techniques to sell, sell, sell, that he has no inner strength with which to meet a crisis. Successful entertainers, sales people, media personalities, and politicians often develop great skills of self-projection, and of pleasing others at the expense of developing strong private interests and a true inner peace built on self-knowledge. It is very hard for politicians to draw the line between their private and public lives, especially in the television era, but unless a politician has a great deal of self-knowledge and introspective strength, trouble can easily arise. The pace and lifestyle on Parliament Hill soon exploit one's weaknesses. The politician who has perfected the skill of pleasing others and who has worked so hard at projecting the consummate public image at the expense of inner strength courts disaster. It is, sadly, an all too frequent occurrence.

Once in Ottawa, contacting the whip's office to examine and choose House of Commons committee assignments reminded me of my freshman year at Mount Allison when I selected my courses at the registrar's office. The only real difference lay in my sad and ultimate conclusion that the freshman-year courses were significantly more meaningful than the committee work in Ottawa would prove to be.

Soon after Parliament got under way, I was appointed to a seat on the Estimates Committee, examining current budgetary estimates. We sat throughout the summer months, often on Saturday mornings, under the able chairmanship of Arthur Smith, the member for Calgary South. Ottawa gets extremely humid in the summer. There was no air-conditioning in the Centre Block, and we were working in a virtual steam bath. The committee first examined the estimates of the Department of National Defence. When, during my cross-examination, I asked why the estimated cost of a frigate had doubled by the time it was finally launched, an irritated admiral questioned my sense of patriotism. Our report was made and submitted to the minister of National Defence, George Pearkes, but ministers are not obliged to accept such recommendations, and they were largely ignored by Pearkes and his officials.

These committee hearings proved to be next to useless. While much still remains to be done to strengthen the role of parliamentary committees, the committee sitting and travelling through the summer recess of 1985 on the question of "Star Wars" and free trade with the United States did a first-class job. Mulroney seems serious in his intention to reform the system, and has already accepted many of the recommendations of the McGrath Committee on Parliamentary Reform. The role or careers of private members should be substantially enhanced because of this initiative, recommending, among other things, increased powers of parliamentary committees.

Unlike their counterparts in Washington, our parliamentary committees are ineffective forums lacking adequate research back-up and expertise. When I testified with Ralph Nader on the question of car safety before the Senate Commerce Committee of Congress in the late winter of 1966, it was easy to see that there had been a great deal of expert research available to the committee, that it had real powers and was taken seriously. In Canada, the recommendations of parliamentary committees are usually shelved and ignored by ministers and their staff. Some members skilfully use the committees as publicity forums to influence public opinion, but this tends to be the exception. I found it hard to take committee work seriously under the prevailing handicaps and circumstances. Members were stuck into parliamentary committees to keep them busy and out of the hair of the bureaucrats and the ministers who are running the show. Like children thrust into playpens to keep them "out of the way," members of Parliament are directed into committees where too often they mistake frenzied activity for the exercise of power. Members of Parliament, like their pitiful counterparts in the normally toothless and powerless Senate, scurry around "the Hill" with documents neatly placed under their arms, pretending to effect change, while the bureaucrats smile with self-satisfaction and ministers to on their merry way. The illusion persists, and the power of self-deception knows no bounds.

I had set up my constituency office in Knowlton, where the phone never stopped ringing, the mail poured in, and constituents literally lined up at my front door to see me. Working hard as a back-bencher and solving constituents' problems was a first-class training ground where I would learn and understand the workings of government and how to deal with the bureaucracy and government departments.

Open warfare broke out between the governor of the Bank of Canada, James Coyne, and the Diefenbaker government during the late winter of 1960 and the following spring. To most members of the Conservative caucus, James Coyne was at best a closet Liberal. The governor, in a series of speeches, publicly attacked the government for its alleged fiscal irresponsibility. In December 1959, addressing the Investment Dealers' Association in Toronto, he said: "No economy as advanced as ours should allow itself to be moulded into a pattern of employment which is dependent for any extended period on capital expenditures financed by foreign money-borrowing on such a scale."

By the following October, however, Coyne's statements had become notably stronger. Speaking to the annual meeting of the Canadian Chamber of Commerce in Calgary, he said:

> We cannot expect to go on indefinitely buying goods and services from abroad in amounts greatly in excess of our exports, that is, buying on credit on a scale which requires large further increases in our foreign debt. We must, therefore, face the prospect of suffering at some stage a major restriction in the supply of goods and services available for consumption and for expansion of capital facilities in Canada — or else we must set about providing for ourselves an amount of goods and services made in Canada through the employment of Canadians, in replacement of the supply from outside, upon which we have been so heavily dependent for the past decade.
>
> In my view our present unemployment cannot be cured by blunderbuss methods of overall larger-scale monetary expansion and deficit finance.

The debate raged on between Coyne and the government, the former charging government interference in monetary policy. Don Fleming's riposte was that the governor had interfered in the government's fiscal policy. The minister touched upon the situation in the House on June 26:

> Until the autumn of 1959, the Governor had not made a practice of making public speeches, but at that time he began to do so. For the next year and a half, he made them with increasing force, frequency and fervour. Never was I or any other member of the government consulted at any time in any respect whatever in regard to the making of those speeches or their contents.
>
> They quickly attracted public attention, which increased with each of those public utterances, principally because they were devoted almost entirely to fiscal, not monetary policy and thus entered upon one of

the most controversial subjects in the whole political spectrum. The Governor did not directly attack the government, but it was not long before the government was bearing the full weight of his criticisms and strictures.

He contended time and time again with ever increasing vehemence that the country was suffering from wrong fiscal policies and the absence of needed fiscal programs. Such, under our constitutional system, Mr. Speaker, are the responsibilities of the government, not the responsibilities of the Bank of Canada.

Coyne's resignation was demanded on May 30, and, in a letter to Fleming dated June 9, he stated: "One reason you gave why the government would not approve my reappointment was that statements in public speeches I have made had turned out to be embarrassing to the government and were being used by their opponents in Parliament and elsewhere for political purposes. You first spoke to me about this matter on March 18th last, and I have not made any public speeches since."

A second, more direct complaint against Coyne was introduced by Fleming in his June 26 speech: "In the winter of 1957–58, I conveyed to him [Coyne] a request for an easing of the requirements respecting the liquidity reserves of chartered banks. That request, which was designed by the government to ease tight money, was rejected by the governor firmly and angrily."

It is not hard to imagine how Coyne would feel about subsequent events, when the Trudeau administration, and particularly John Turner, put pressure on the Bank of Canada to get the printing presses rolling and increase the money supply.

The recourse by which the government sought to declare Coyne's post vacant was Bill C-114. The opposition asked for a joint committee to hear both sides of the question. Their argument was that only Parliament could fire Coyne. The debate took an ugly turn when Coyne's pension rights were discussed. Fleming made a statement about this matter in the House on June 14:

> Prior to February 15, 1960, Mr. Coyne under present circumstances of age and service would have been entitled on retirement this year to a life pension of slightly less than $12,000 per annum. As the result of a by-law passed by the Board [of Governors of the Bank] that day he claims to have acquired immediate entitlement of a life pension of $25,000 per annum on retirement this year at age approximately 50 years.
>
> The government was notified of this by-law and the Governor did not publish it in the Canada Gazette until this week. The government became aware of the enactment of this by-law only this spring. The government, as I informed him at the meeting on May 30, considers that the Governor was lacking in a sense of responsibility in keeping with his high office, in accepting an additional benefit worth $13,000 per annum for life without ensuring that the matter was brought to the attention of the government.

Coyne, in his June 9 letter, had more to say about his removal by the government:

> The sudden and unexplained demand for my resignation on May 30, the appearance of haste and urgency, and the blackmailing tactics used, suggested that the present government had a plan to call a snap election, without a budget, or perhaps immediately after the budget speech was made, and subvert the Bank of Canada under a new governor of their own choosing to

assist them in financing expenditures and programs not authorized by Parliament.

I was warned about this danger by a man whose opinions I value and who said in such circumstances the governor of the Bank would have a duty not to resign. In the absence of any other rational explanation of the government's action, it may yet be proved that electoral intentions were the real purpose of the move to get rid of me. The delay in bringing in the budget, and the fact that the budget was rewritten after my statements appeared, are further indications that ulterior designs underlay the plan to get me out of the way.

Bill C-114 passed and Coyne was out, but by the time Louis Rasminsky was appointed governor on July 24, both the government and the Bank of Canada had been inevitably hurt. The political infighting created public cynicism, and Canada lost prestige abroad. In the September 1961 issue of *Canadian Business*, William Thoms wrote:

> Since May 30 when the Canadian government asked former governor Coyne for his resignation, the bond and money markets had continued to operate on their own momentum but without direction.
> For almost two months, while the case of Her Majesty's Canadian Government vs. James Coyne raged in Parliament and press, the Canadian public waited, listened and watched with mounting anxiety and embarrassment. It was the kind of anxiety ship's passengers feel when told the vessel has lost its rudder . . . .
> The most alarming aspect of the Coyne episode was the veritable chasm it revealed between the Bank of Canada and the Department of Finance, and with all of the thousands of words thrown into the controversy the

public was still left to wonder who, if anyone, was calling the tune on monetary policy. To many Canadians it was a national embarrassment. Canada — with its solid-as-a-rock banking system, with a former governor of its central bank whom foreign governments seek out for advice and help on national banking problems, a country which American editorial writers frequently hold up to their government as one which follows the path of fiscal and monetary rectitude — had shown to the world a less-than-solid grip on a vital aspect of national administration.

Individual bureaucrats are normally fine and dedicated public servants. If they have undue power and influence, it's largely because the "representatives of the people" have abdicated their fundamental responsibilities. I am convinced that unresponsive, collective bureaucratic control is not unlike the totalitarian rule of the monarchs in England before the establishment of parliamentary democracy. The solution to this dilemma involves one big difference. In the era of all-powerful beings, the answer was to cut off their heads. We can't do that with "pleasant" and "nice" public servants. The problem and its solution are nevertheless just as urgent as they were hundreds of years ago, especially when contemporary government is all-pervasive in our lives. In 1983, when Brian Mulroney took over the Progressive Conservative party, he had little or no understanding of the bureaucracy and the workings of government; he had not served his apprenticeship. Surgeons must serve long and arduous internships before operating on their patients. By allowing Mulroney to take short cuts and operate on Canada before he paid his dues, my party committed a disgraceful disservice to Canada, and we are still paying the price.

A case in point involves Iraq's former ambassador to the United States, who has been granted landed immigrant status in Canada. Mohamed al-Mashat was a personal friend of Saddam Hussein's, and on the assumption that there was no ministerial or prime-ministerial interference in this matter, Mashat was let into Canada by the bureaucrats, who did not bother to keep their political masters abreast of developments. This case is symbolic of what is happening under the present government, which has trouble controlling the bureaucracy.

Unelected officials around the prime minister's office and the bureaucracy have taken over as never before. This must not be permitted to continue. Canadians should not be asked to make unnecessary sacrifices as their leaders get training on the job.

12

MINORITY GOVERNMENT 1979
"THAT WON'T FLY, MR. MINISTER"

By the time the 1979 campaign got under way, I had already fought eight general elections since 1957. Between the years 1957 and 1980, I would fight ten general elections, averaging nearly one every two years. This testament to our political instability produced no fewer than six minority governments. Members of Parliament seemed to be constantly running for office, leaving policy matters and the running of the country largely in the hands of the entrenched Ottawa bureaucracy.

The Tory campaign in Québec in the spring of 1979 was a total disaster. Since becoming leader in 1976, Joe Clark had done his very best to build up the party fortunes in Québec. On the surface, Mulroney and his Québec entourage would seem to have supported Clark and his efforts in Québec. Mulroney's support and enthusiasm were lukewarm at best. I was, nevertheless, re-elected along with Roch LaSalle from Joliette. We would be the only two members from Québec in the new Tory caucus.

A few days after the election, I received a phone call from the prime minister–elect at my house in Knowlton. He informed me that he wanted me to join his cabinet and to meet with him the next week in Ottawa. I appeared at his suite at the Four Seasons hotel at the appointed time. He was in a relaxed mood, but obviously unhappy that the Québec results had denied him a majority government. He then asked me to become his minister of state for Social Programmes. This was a new post and I had no idea what was involved. Was it a new superministry involving social programs largely from Health and Welfare and many other ministries or was it just a ministry of state, low in the traditional order of things. Clark told me to consult with the deputy minister of Health and Welfare to sort things out. Neverthe-less, I left him that day somewhat confused as to what my future responsibilities would be.

June 4, 1979, was the day set for the new government to take over. Clark and his new ministers-to-be and their families walked down the road under a sunny sky to the entrance of Rideau Hall and it would be hard to imagine a happier group. Laughter and greetings were the order of the day. When we reached Rideau Hall, Pierre Trudeau, informally dressed in sports clothing, had just left the front entrance. He had given his resignation to the Governor General, and I could detect a carefree air about him. It was easy to see that he was working on his new beard.

Trudeau jumped into the silver Mercedes convertible that he had brought to Ottawa with him as a bachelor after the 1965 elections. The top was down. Before speeding off, he waved at me and yelled out his good wishes. I went over to his car, shook hands, and wished him well. My constituency secretary, Margaret Macey, had come up to Ottawa for the celebrations. She witnessed the event and, suffering from a mild case of Trudeaumania, was ecstatic.

On the day of my swearing-in at Government House, the press wanted an answer. They wanted to know the exact nature of my responsibilities. "What's your job?" a voice cried out from the crowd of journalists surrounding me at the

Rideau Hall reception. I had a hard time masking my uncertainty, and the press weren't to be fooled.

An incident took place the next day that I shall always cherish and never forget.

In 1945, when I was seventeen years old, after a high-school visit to Parliament Hill, I informed a security guard at the entrance to the House of Commons, with typical teenage brashness, that I would be back in a few years as a full-fledged member of Parliament. After my swearing-in at the age of twenty-nine in the spring of 1958, he was there to greet me outside the Speaker's chambers. On the morning after my swearing-in as new minister, before I arrived at my office at the West Block on Parliament Hill, my old friend awaited my arrival, some thirty-four years after my high-school visit. Whether ministers like it or not, security guards salute them as they pass by in the corridors. "Let me be the first to salute you!" he exclaimed as he raised his hand to his head. He was, and we laughed together.

My first task was to put together a good ministerial staff. This isn't always easy. Each minister is allotted a specific budget for his own staff. Ministerial appointments are obviously important. In my view, they should strike a solid balance between "a knowledge of the civil service and how it works," on the one hand, and what is often referred to as "political smarts," on the other hand. I chose Brian Derrick as my executive assistant. His family came from my part of the world, and were party supporters. He had worked for the Department of National Revenue in Ottawa for a number of years in relatively senior positions.

My instructions to my new executive assistant were clear. He was not to fall into the trap of becoming simply a mouthpiece for the bureaucracy and its agenda, as often happens in Ottawa. Executive assistants, now called chiefs of staff, rub shoulders much more often with the civil servants than with politicians, and easily fall prey to the temptation of expressing the former's point of view. I well remember this occurring when Diefenbaker governed between 1957 and 1963. Executive assistants were more than prone to lecture MPs on the rules of the bureaucracy. Breathing humanism and equitable discretion into the labyrinth of government was neither their preoccupation nor their forte. The combination of such an executive assistant, a powerful deputy minister, and a weak minister normally spelled disaster.

As we prepared to settle into my new ministry, it was obvious that the number-one priority was to define my new responsibilities. Derrick and I set out on the quest.

The press continued to question me before reporting, "Grafftey has little or nothing to do." I found it incomprehensible that neither the Privy Council Office or Prime Minister's Office had defined clearly the role of ministers of state.

In my view, the relationship between such ministers and their senior minister should not be left to the two of them to work out. During the latter part of June and the beginning of July, I conferred with Jim Gillies, a senior policy adviser to the prime minister and subsequently with the prime minister himself in an attempt to put order into things. Over at Health and Welfare, policy suggestions from Crombie and me were met with the same theme song from the deputy minister, Bruce Lawson — "That won't fly, Mr. Minister." Policy emanating from the outside, including from the minister himself, was looked upon with scepticism by senior bureaucrats. The NIH (Not Invented Here) syndrome and its bias was in full force. It was finally agreed that I would be responsible for pension policy, including improving the Canada Pension Plan. I got to work with my staff and relevant departmental officials, under Del Lynseth, assistant deputy minister, preparing for the new session of Parliament, which would begin in September.

Once my new responsibilities for pension policy were more or less defined, department officials were slated to brief me. I assume my briefing sessions were not unlike those given to other ministers. They involved a thorough indoctrination on the "bureaucratic agenda" and procedures. As long as a new minister is being briefed on how things are done, he or she cannot get in anybody's way or, what is worse, assume control of his or her department. Of course, a certain amount of briefing is necessary. In my own case, things went too far. One day, I found myself in the east end of Ottawa where a young fellow in blue jeans planned to instruct me for a few hours on how the computers processed pension cheques. I put a stop to it. My briefing came to an abrupt end.

The press were made aware of my new role, but were as surprised as I was when Crombie, during a trip to Prince Edward Island, made a major policy statement on pensions. A number of journalists questioned me on this turn of events, and I was reliably informed that Stanley Knowles, the NDP critic for pensions, was about to exploit this confusion on the floor of the House once the session got under way. In a subsequent phone conversation with the prime minister, I informed him of this state of affairs and frankly stated, with no criticism of Crombie, that I didn't feel he wanted a minster of state attached to his department, and that his deputy minister was surely opposed to it. When the prime minister transferred the deputy minister to other responsibilities a few days later, I thought it a possible harbinger of improved circumstances. I was wrong.

During this period, I carried out some specific duties at the prime minister's request. The child tax credit, as it applied before 1979, involved some negative political implications in that the opposition could claim, with reason, that a sort of means test was applied before recipients could receive the tax break. I conferred with the minister of National Revenue, Walter Baker, and his officials in order to rectify the situation and simplify the tax forms. We brought the matter to a successful conclusion.

Apart from departmental work, cabinet meetings were, for me, a revelation and challenge. Three matters disturbed me in that they surely enhanced the power and control of the bureaucracy. The first involved the number of bureaucrats who attended cabinet meetings. In all fairness, during what is termed "discussion" on the political agenda, bureaucrats normally left the cabinet room. Nevertheless, during the routine discussion of matters brought before cabinet committees, bureaucrats often outnumber the ministers in attendance. I understand that a particular minister introducing a specific measure before cabinet needs to be accompanied by senior officials from his or her departments. Yet even when questions not affecting their departments were before the cabinet committee, ministers would appear with a coterie of their officials. Officials from the Department of Finance were everywhere, sitting in on most cabinet committee sessions. On one occasion, a Finance official supposedly attended cabinet on behalf of his minister. I could not help wondering whether or not the minister himself knew what was going on.

Another matter was brought to my attention, namely, that deputy ministers had regular meetings among themselves. Insofar as ministers and their deputies should have a broad overview of government policy, this is a good thing. But there is and continues to be a reverse side to the coin. It involves confidentiality. While gregarious politicians leak to the press, so do secretive bureaucrats who don't like what is going on in cabinet. What is more, they leak to the opposition parties as well. By frequently attending cabinet meetings in great numbers and by organizing themselves on a regular basis, the collective bureaucracy can easily sidetrack or defeat any specific ministerial initiative that does not fall into line with their agenda. This leads to another consideration. The cabinet agenda, or the agendas of cabinet committees, are largely made up in the Privy Council Office (PCO). This is the senior bureaucratic coordinating arm of government as opposed to the Prime Minister's Office (PMO), which is the senior political grouping of political officials named at the discretion of the prime minister. Unless a prime minister is eternally vigilant, which cannot realistically be expected, the agenda is controlled far too well by the PCO, and individual ministers find their pet projects are not even up for discussion. Of course the prime minister himself can veto discussions of any ministerial initiative he doesn't want to hear about.

John Diefenbaker once pointed out to me the powers he had, some of which he never knew were there. He omitted to mention the power he had in setting the cabinet agenda. When I brought this to his attention, he feigned surprise with a twinkle in his eyes and his usual incomparable chuckle.

If the reader regrets that I am not fleshing out these considerations with "live" examples from my experience he or she must realize that I am bound by the rules of cabinet as well as caucus secrecy. Let future historians, if they wish, flesh out my conclusions by referring to the "archives."

One of the most extreme examples that comes to mind, though, involves the Cuban Missile Crisis in 1962. At that time I was Finance minister George Nowlan's parliamentary secretary. The cabinet was in total deadlock over the question whether our forces should be put on "emergency alert." Diefenbaker and his Defence minister, Douglas Harkness, were barely speaking, and no cabinet policy on the issue was forthcoming. While it would be ridiculous, on my part, to suggest that Canada could ever be subjected to a "military coup," what I witnessed at the time seemed incredible. Without any clear cabinet directive, the chief of staff did put our forces on "emergency alert." I have no reason to believe things have changed. Under similar circumstances, we could easily have a repetition of this scenario.

Then there was the question of cabinet documents. These involve the briefing work that each minister must bring home each night before cabinet meetings. They touch upon matters not only affecting the minister's department, but in all other matters to be brought before cabinet. If a minister wants to participate intelligently in cabinet debate, it is obvious that he or she must read and digest these documents. Thus, their importance. Cabinet documents are supposedly TOP SECRET, and are handed over to the minister with some ceremony. "FOR THE MINISTER'S EYES ONLY" are buzzwords in Ottawa as are "PERSONAL AND CONFIDENTIAL." The minister might properly return cabinet documents to his or her chief of staff, but in fact their contents are no secret among much of the bureaucracy and, at times, some of the press. Who gets to see cabinet documents constitutes one of Ottawa's better guessing games.

It soon became apparent to me that the vast majority of cabinet briefing papers were badly drawn up and normally expressed the preconceived bias of the bureaucrats. Most of the documents given to me were in appalling disarray and far too long. A good précis writer could easily have presented the pith and substance of recommendations and saved me and other ministers valuable time. To my consternation and amazement, the bureaucratic recommendations often presented only the bureaucrats' side of the story. Let us consider a hypothetical example: a choice between the government buying one or another kind of airplane. The bureaucracy would make the choice, and flatter the ministers by letting them decide what colour to paint the plane, and so it went. Unlike the White House, where presidential advisers take advice from the private sector to counterbalance judgements made by individual departmental secretaries and their officials, Canada has no such remedy. Our bureaucrats are disdainful of outside advice. As we have already seen, Walter Gordon, Lester Pearson's hapless minister of Finance, learned this when he called in outside advisers to help him with his first budget. Gordon's deputy minister disagreed with the nationalistic thrust of the budget and pulled the rug from under his minister. Finance officials who were normally present in the House of Commons gallery to guide their minister through the budget debate dismissed themselves, leaving Gordon to flounder.

My relationship with Prime Minister Clark was always friendly, informal, and frank, although I guess he regretted my outbursts and confrontations with the party hierarchy in Québec, and with Mulroney.

Admittedly, I could have been more diplomatic with Mulroney and his friends, who seemed to me to be extremely patronizing towards rural people. I believed in building from the grass roots up. They had an "élitist" attitude of building from the top down. I didn't believe it would work then, and it surely isn't working now. This issue was at the heart of my confrontations with Mulroney and his gang. His gang included friends such as Lucien Bouchard, now leading the Bloc Québécois, and Richard Holden, a member of the English Rights Equality Party in Québec.

On this basis, in a private conversation during the summer of 1979, I gave Clark my point of view about the state of cabinet documents, their potential for political disaster, and their discouragement of initiatives from sources other than the civil service. The Not Invented Here syndrome among the bureaucrats was fraught with danger for a minority government skating on thin political ice.

In mid-summer, I attempted, on many occasions, to improve my relations with the party hierarchy in Montréal. I had often likened them to the British generals in the First World War, comparing their political tactics to the stupidity of the trench-warfare tactics of the British military commanders. A phone call to Mulroney proved relatively useless. I sensed by his tone of voice that, if bridges had not been burned, they were in a state of near collapse.

When John Diefenbaker died in August, I marched in the funeral procession to Christ Church Cathedral in Ottawa with Pierre Trudeau. Upon arriving at the cathedral, I saw Mulroney on the sidewalk by the entrance to the church. Without extending his hand, he glared at me icily with a "meet one of the Montréal generals" look. My efforts were in vain. Mulroney and his entourage could not really accept the fact that my friend Joe Clark was prime minister.

While walking to the cathedral with Trudeau, I cast my mind back over the past few days. At noon the week before, rain had been falling heavily outside my West Block office. As I looked out of my office window, I could see Diefenbaker was standing alone when an aide came out, apparently to tell him that the West Block cafeteria was closed and he could not eat there. He looked sad and bewildered, and went off with his aide. I noticed a certain depression surrounding the Chief during the summer months. He had lost his beloved Olive and was surely suffering. In the Centre Block dining room, I would often see him eating alone and would leave my table to join him, sometimes taking a guest or two with me. Naturally, he felt more than a little left out of things and wasn't overly enthusiastic in his praise of Joe Clark.

Seeing Diefenbaker eating alone reminded me of a similar experience back in the summer of 1957. Louis St. Laurent had just been defeated as prime minister and he, too, would often sit alone at a table in the Centre Block restaurant. Before the 1957 elections, he had just completed a world tour and was totally exhausted. He had suggested on many occasions that the Liberal Party find a new leader and prime minister, but nobody would hear of it, and he was persuaded to run one more time. In defeat, like Diefenbaker, he ate alone.

Politics is a cruel game, but I felt then, as I do now, that there should be at least an informal protocol that dictates that ex–prime ministers don't sit alone in their old age in public parliamentary dining rooms.

Diefenbaker's funeral was a great event, and reminded me of the pageantry surrounding Winston Churchill's service and burial. I was not surprised: after Lester Pearson's funeral, some of us remarked to Diefenbaker that it was a rather lovely event, to which he replied, "Wait till you see mine!"

By the time the full cabinet met in Québec City in the late summer, I had truly adjusted to the demands of participating in cabinet work. I was able to devote much of my time to cabinet debate. Clark's leadership in cabinet was superb, and I hope I made a contribution in the give-and-take with him and my colleagues. In mid-September, Brian Derrick, my executive assistant, informed me that a rumour was circulating that I was slated for a promotion in a cabinet shuffle to take place before the opening of the House.

On Thanksgiving weekend, I headed down to Higgins Beach, near Portland, Maine, to be with my family and friends at The Breakers Inn, facing the sea. At lunch, Rodney Laughton, the owner, came to the dining room to inform me that the Prime Minister's Office was on the line. I had already received a call from Derrick, telling me to expect a call relative to a cabinet promotion. The prime minister knew I had done much work in opposition in the field of science policy. Once on the phone, he asked me to take over the ministry of Science and Technology. This portfolio was both a ministry of State for Science and Technology throughout the government (MOSST) and a full operating ministry overseeing the

National Research Council (NRC) and the Natural Sciences and Engineering Research Council (NSERC). The Science Council of Canada, an independent agency like the Economic Council, would report to Parliament through me. While those working at the National Research Council were not civil servants in the true sense of the word under the Public Service Act, the prime minister agreed that I should develop a deputy-ministerial relationship with Bill Schneider, then president of the NRC. The principal thrust of NSERC was and is to fund scientific and technological research at our universities. The prime minister asked me to meet him at 2:00 p.m. on Monday, Thanksgiving Day, at 24 Sussex Drive, before going over to the Governor General's for the swearing-in at Rideau Hall. I was met at 24 Sussex by an official from the Prime Minister's Office, who briefed me on the swearing-in procedure before I met with the prime minister in the private living quarters. Once there, the first thing that struck me was the breath-taking view of the Gatineau Hills across the Rideau River. I had the sensation of being suspended over the stone cliffs by the side of the river. From this vantage point, you can look east and west up and down this magnificent flow of water. The prime minister's mother was there, as well as his brother and family. I had visited their home town of High River, Alberta, on previous occasions, and we all had a good chat before setting out with the prime minister for Rideau Hall.

Newspaper, radio, and television reporters had over the weekend anticipated at least a minor cabinet shuffle. I became somewhat suspicious that I was the only minister involved after having met alone with the prime minister at Sussex Drive and being the only minister to accompany him to Rideau Hall. Once there, we could see scores of journalists crowding around the main entrance in anticipation, hurling the usual barrage of questions at Clark and myself. We proceeded to a private study at the end of the hall, where preparations had been finalized for the swearing-in. They included beverages and eats. Greeting us were Marcel Masse, the new clerk of the Privy Council; Brian Derrick; and half a dozen members of my immediate staff, who lined the walls in the study as unobtrusively as possible. They were all decked out in their Sunday best. It is hard to believe, but bureaucratic intransigence and insensitivity were in full swing, even relating to such a matter as a swearing-in ceremony. Esmond Butler, an aide to the Government General, coolly informed me that my staff members couldn't be there for the swearing-in and would have to leave. Whether this decision was based on strict protocol or was merely a discretionary flexing of muscles, I shall never know. At any rate, I was miffed and could not hide my annoyance as my staff had worked incredibly hard over the past months and were a large part of the reason for my promotion. My staff duly left the study with disappointment etched on their faces. The remaining small group, including the prime minister, awaited the arrival of the Ed Schreyer, then Governor General. I was escorted, alone, down the hall to a larger room by an amiable and cheerful steward to the Governor General. I had met and talked with him on many previous occasions during receptions at Rideau Hall. I expressed to him my pique at the exclusion of my staff from the swearing-in, and he seemed more than sympathetic. At any rate, the original decision to exclude them was obviously not based on any sacrosanct principle of protocol, for as I paced up and down the big room awaiting "my call," I could hear a lot of quiet chuckling in the outside hall. I could see from the open door the steward ushering my staff quickly back to the study. They all gave me a mischievous wave as they went by. In no time, my call came. The oath was administered by Marcel Masse, the only ministerial oath he would have a chance to administer during the term of our minority government. As my staff stood with their backs to the wall, in the small study, the prime minister and Governor General solemnly flanked us and it was all over. We chatted informally, the champagne was poured before toasting and wishing me good luck. As Governor General Schreyer, the prime minister, and I approached the main entrance, the press corps awaited us. One fellow yelled out, "Is Grafftey going to be busier in his new portfolio? Will he stop complaining about not having enough to do?" The prime minister, smiling, handled the question. We stepped out into the sunlight bathing the beautiful grounds and the autumn colours around Rideau Hall, before going our separate ways. I was about to face new challenges. For me, a big dream had come true, and I was happy about it.

During the time of John Kennedy's thousand days as president of the United States, he initiated a practice I have always felt had a beneficial and sobering effect. He would call, at any time, one public servant out of the many thousands, at any level in a department over any question, big or small. It could involve for example, a lost pension file that had caused delays and prejudice for an individual citizen who should have been drawing a pension but was not. The astonished pension officer in, let us say, Phoenix, Arizona, would react in total disbelief when he heard the president's voice on the other end of the line. I am told that George Bush has reintroduced the practice, which is meant to keep public servants on their toes. I told Denis Hudon, the deputy minister at MOSST, that I intended to follow this procedure from time to time in my new department. I cannot say that my intentions were met with applause and enthusiasm; bypassing deputy ministers in Ottawa to contact individual public servants is not encouraged. One thing that came to my attention as I got my feet under my desk caused me great consternation. It involved my letter book. Observers of the parliamentary scene often witness ministers entering the House with a number of thick green books under their arms. These books contain departmental letters to be signed in answer to letters and queries. I was shocked when presented with my first series of books. Some of the letters I was typically asked to sign were in reply to correspondence received from individual citizens three and four months before. An example would be that, on August 25, I would find a letter prepared for my signature in my book, reading: "Dear Mr. Smith, In answer to your letter of May 3" I was enraged and told my executive assistant and senior officials to rectify the problem, saying that I wanted letters answered within two weeks of their receipt. I was told that some of the answers needed a lot of researching, and that there just wasn't enough staff to meet my request. I replied that staff should be allotted from another section of the ministry, only to be informed that regulations wouldn't permit my request to be fulfilled. "What regulations?" I inquired. When a sensible reply didn't seem to be forthcoming, I informed all present at the meeting that I would refuse to sign letters replying to correspondence from taxpayers that was more than two weeks old. That seemed to do it, and after considerable whining, my demands were met.

As already pointed out, regulations can distort many things in Ottawa. Former ministers, both Progressive Conservative and Liberal, told me on more than one occasion that the central proposals of their intended legislation were altered and totally distorted by the interpretation applied to regulations attached to the legislation. Such was surely the case when, under Trudeau, Labour minister Bryce Mackasey's amendments to the Unemployment Insurance Act virtually turned the act into a massive social-insurance scheme.

As we prepared to meet the House of Commons, I refined a scheme that other ministers had used before me. On regular occasions, I asked my staff to prepare a series of questions that the opposition would likely put to me during Question Period in the Commons. They prepared the questions and answers on a series of cards, often with statistics and background information. The cards were duly indexed and put into a book for me to take into the House. I called them my "idiot cards." The procedure worked well. Once the session got under way, I kept the book on my lap. As a question was being put to me from across the floor of the House, I would find the relevant card. Rarely would I have to take a question on "notice," and inform my questioner at a later date. After a series of questions directed at me in the House one day, the prime minister came to my desk to congratulate me and smiled when I showed him my idiot cards. This procedure proved to be a first-class way to keep on top of things in my department and encourage my officials.

Soon after I took over my new portfolio, I realized that I would be working with some capable and devoted public servants, such as Bill Schneider of the National Research Council and Denis Hudon, secretary of MOSST. Bill Schneider worked bravely with me under a terrible personal handicap. His wife was suffering from the last stages of cancer. Through no fault of these men, science policy was in disarray. Since the creation of the department, no one minister had remained for much more than a year. A series of ministers came and went, and morale was low, not only within government ranks, but within the science community at large from coast to coast.

The fact is that in Canada, successive prime ministers, especially during the past thirty years, have shifted ministers far too often. In many cases an individual minister gets a lever on his or her ministry only to be shuffled post-haste to ministerial responsibilities. Then another greenhorn takes over the responsibilities and begins learning on the job. Far too often, ministers are not really equipped with a "policy agenda" for their respective departments, and the bureaucrats, suspicious of outside advice, take over and develop policy. The result is that the minister, often preoccupied with broad political considerations, rubber-stamps the former minister's decisions. It doesn't take long for most ministers to be brought to heel, as permanent officials are only too happy to run the show. Public servants are not always at fault: the sad state of affairs can be laid at the door of ministers, who far too often abdicate their fundamental responsibilities.

While my own senior officials were at first more than reluctant to receive "outside advice" relating to science policy, I talked to them in this regard and felt sure we were on the road to having a sound and solid policy mix based on a good working relationship between my officials and the science community in the private sector.

In many ways, my tasks were made easier by the make-up of the three councils relating to my ministry. Very often, distinguished citizens from the science community in the private sector served on them. Within two weeks of my new appointment as minister, I met with the members of the National Research Council and listened with great interest to their views. I thought it important to tell them that I felt one of my central roles as minister was to explain the long-term goals of "science" to the community at large so that Canadian science would have its rightful place in the sky. This had not been done in the past. For every dollar we were spending in Canada on research and development, our major trading partners were spending three to four. We were killing the goose that could lay the golden egg.

As I prepared my departmental initiatives, policy and otherwise, one general consideration was firmly in my mind. I knew that having departmental backing and enthusiasm for our goals and objectives was not enough. Experience taught me that such goals and objectives were easily defeated if a minister didn't coordinate them with other ministerial colleagues who might be affected. Normally, close coordination and cooperation with the Prime Minister's Office, the Privy Council Office, Treasury Board, and Finance are needed. Ministers who have neglected this often wonder why their pet projects died at the gate.

There is yet another consideration I was aware of. Modern deputy ministers are very often "generalists," in the true sense of the word. They rarely, if ever, veto initiatives prepared by officials lower down in the hierarchy. Once a lower official prepares an initiative, its recommendations are invariably cast in stone, rarely to be overturned as they move up the ladder. That was why I insisted that I have access to them and they to me, although they were normally accompanied by senior officials, including the deputy minister, while meeting in my office. Unfortunately, as I have discovered over the last number of years, all too often this state of affairs exists in large corporations in the private sector. Many big corporations have bureaucratic constipation. Chief executive officers too often virtually delegate themselves out of their rightful roles and become a rubber stamp for policy decisions that should be theirs. Creative policy, long-term and otherwise, suffers or is non-existent.

In one case, Trudeau flexed his opposition muscles. The matter involved the Iran hostage question. My stepbrother, Eldon Black, recently our ambassador to the Vatican, had briefed the prime minister and Flora MacDonald, our External Affairs minister, on the situation. Previously, our ambassador in Iran, Ken Taylor, had sought and received permission from Clark and MacDonald to hide and house the Americans in our Iranian embassy. They were fully aware that U.S. officials were being given asylum and protection in our embassy in Teheran.

Under the circumstances, it was normal for the leader of the opposition to be briefed on the details of this affair. Trudeau was fully aware that U.S. officials were in hiding in our Iranian embassy. Yet this knowledge did not stop him from attacking the government day after day in the House. Flora MacDonald sat in her seat, biting her tongue, in stunned disbelief as Trudeau went on the attack, accusing the government of doing nothing to alleviate the situation.

Prime Minister Clark took seriously the part research and development should have in government initiatives. He and many of his ministers would give much-needed support to me and my officials in our work. In the fall of 1979, one major problem faced us. From coast to coast, at the university level, research and development were in a perilous state. Lack of funding and a serious shortage of competent personnel on our campuses plagued the science community. Equipment in our university labs was in disrepair, old and out of date. The situation was critical. Working with senior officials at my ministry, we prepared a five-year funding plan to be presented to cabinet. Our universities needed some sort of stability in their future planning and, while government cannot normally endow funds in perpetuity, such an arrangement, with concrete funding guaranteed for the first year, was a major move forward. For the remaining four years, the government signalled its specific funding intentions.

Governments must avoid funding in perpetuity. In the summer of 1958 Dr. Wilder Penfield and some of his senior colleagues from the world-famous Montreal Neurological Institute met with me in Ottawa. I had arranged a meeting with them and Prime Minister Diefenbaker, together with his minister of Health and Welfare, Waldo Martieth. Penfield wanted the federal authority to endow the institute over a number of years. At our meeting with the prime minister, Martieth pointed out the impossibility of committing funds in this manner in perpetuity. Penfield's consolation was a substantial one-year grant.

For the first time since the creation of the Science ministry, the prime minister named me, as minister, to sit in on senior cabinet committees, namely, the Economic and Social Affairs Committees. This posting boosted the morale of my senior officials and gave me greater access to the decision-making process, where I could plead the case for science. After much hard work and preparation, the five-year plan was presented to cabinet committee, the inner cabinet, and ultimately the full cabinet. For a while, it was touch and go, as I had no little difficulty in getting the matter put on the cabinet agenda for debate. Undue delay would have easily killed the measure. Our persistence paid off, and the plan was approved. Naturally, the science community was ecstatic. We had made a good beginning. That plan was one of the very few major initiatives of our short-lived minority government.

One matter disturbed me in all of this. Gordon McNab, an able public servant, headed the Natural Sciences and Engineering Research Council. He played a major role in preparing the plan and getting it through. I was led to believe that his job as head of the NSERC would require his full-time efforts if the plan was to be successfully administered and carried out. Some time after its approval, it came to my attention through reliable sources that McNab would give only part-time attention to his NSERC duties. He had accepted another part-time post at Energy, Mines, and Resources. I felt it was entirely incorrect that I, as minister, had not been informed of this. I phoned Marcel Masse, clerk of the Privy Council, and voiced my objections. McNab remained at NSERC on a full-time basis. While McNab was dedicated and able, I couldn't help but feel that a modicum of bureaucratic arrogance and insensitive negligence was involved in this incident.

Ministerial responsibility means just that. No matter how much I or other politicians rail against the powers of entrenched bureaucracies and their undemocratic tendencies, the buck stops at the minister's desk. He or she is responsible. Public servants can't be blamed, at least publicly, when things go wrong. Ultimate responsibility lies in the minister's hands. That is as it should be.

Part Five

Some Unfinished Business

13

A Modern Constitution for Modern Times

Before starting out, I must warn the reader. I believe that it is not too late to save the union. It won't be the union we have known in the past. It will be new and better. Too much positive history has gone into creating Canada. The work of Cartier and Macdonald will not be undone overnight. The current crisis has been exacerbated by weak or non-existent federal leadership, coupled with unprecedented "regionalism." This does not have to and should not continue.

Back in the 1950s, when I was first elected, my French-speaking electors would ask me if I was *un Canadien*. While they were asking, in fact, if I was a French-speaking Canadian, the question had a strong underlying significance. It meant, among other things, that they had a real identification with Canada, often feeling, with reason, that their English-speaking compatriots in Québec were more British than the British. Now, almost thirty years later, the children of those who questioned me ask if I am *un Québécois*. Symbolic of this state of affairs are the sons of two ex-premiers of the province, Daniel Johnson and Jean-Jacques Bertrand. The sons, Pierre-Marc Johnson and Jean-François Bertrand, saw their fathers try to introduce relatively mild legislation to protect the French language in Québec, only to be wounded by the intransigence of Québec's English-speaking minority. Now the sons are active members of the Parti Québécois.

While my riding was not really typical of the rest of Québec, my experience in representing it has largely shaped my views that with leadership and understanding, French and English can co-exist from coast to coast. Let us be certain of one thing. A unilingual French Québec and a unilingual "rest of Canada" is *not* the new Canada I envisage. Such a phenomenon would make the union mean and meaningless. The work ahead, to bring Canada together in a spirit of understanding, cooperation, and unity, will not be easy. It will require time and patience, hard work and application, all carried out in spirit of give and take. Yet if we look at the current situation, we must admit time is not on our side.

The federal/provincial constitutional conference at Victoria, Trudeau's attempts at patriation — excluding Québec — and finally Meech Lake were the last nails in the coffin of a constitutional framework perhaps suited to a bygone age but no longer suitable to meet the demands and realities of a new and exciting Canada. We do not know our strength if we do not know our history. Not forgetting our past, we must start anew.

How many of us have tried to keep an old car on the road, only to be told by the garage mechanic that it's not worth repairing. Scrap it and get a new one. It is thus with our present constitution. Our Fathers of Confederation met 124 years ago under conditions very different from those of the present time. They put partisan political considerations aside. The birth of Canada was a unique act of statesmanship. I am sure those who drafted our initial constitutional document would be the first to recognize that it is no longer suited to contemporary realities. Macdonald and Cartier would wish us well as we go about seeking consensus for a "new constitution."

A MODERN CONSTITUTION FOR MODERN TIMES

The past thirty years, starting with the so called Quiet Revolution in my province, has been a crucial period leading up to the present situation.

Heading a minority government in 1963, Diefenbaker turned thumbs down on any suggestion for a "bilingual and bicultural" commission. He had other things in mind, but was instantly and unfairly labelled "anti-Québec." A year later, with Pearson as prime minister, Jean Lesage and his colleagues coined the slogan *Maîtres chez nous*. He was insisting on opting out of such joint programs as the Canada Pension Plan and Medicare. My instant reaction was to recognize the need for a modern constitution for modern times. As far back as 1964, it was easy to see that no amount of amending formulas to the existing constitution would do the trick. In my subsequent talks with Diefenbaker, I soon discovered what he had in mind, as he encouraged me to speak out for modern constitutional reform. He articulated his views to me on the need for some sort of Estates Générals or constitutional convention in order to start the consultative procedures and national dialogue. All these initiatives would come to an end, as forces within the party would surely bring Diefenbaker down. It is fair to say that Diefenbaker was his own worst enemy and surely hurt his own cause.

At a reception given by Radio-Canada in Montréal in the late fall of Expo year (1967), I was able to say in a short address that it was my hope that francophones living outside Québec would be made to feel as much at home as I, an anglophone, felt within Québec. Little did I know that in a few years, I would be denied freedom of speech by a mean-spirited premier, aided and abetted by a spineless federal prime minister.

There was a good spirit in the land in 1967, and I truly feel it was not entirely illusory. The Québécois until then had a strong nationalist penchant in supporting their provincial governments in Québec while simultaneously electing prime ministers who defended the federal cause.

Soon after my party named Bob Stanfield as leader, in September 1967, Pierre Trudeau was on the scene as prime minister. Over the dead body of Diefenbaker, Stanfield adopted and supported the "two nations" theory. Nobody knew what it meant. One thing is certain: it meant one thing in English and an entirely different thing in French. Undaunted, Stanfield plunged ahead. Mulroney, Marcel Faribeault, and a well-meaning group of Montréal Tory anglos encouraged Stanfield in the conviction that the two-nations doctrine was the best thing since cream cheese. Trudeau took up the challenge, ridiculed Stanfield and his theory, and in the election of June 1968 soundly defeated my party at the polls. The fat was in the fire, and the stage was set for Trudeau's "politics of confrontation." His federal opponents had vacated the playing field, which he now had all to himself. Expo year was euphoric in many ways. Perhaps the spirit of goodwill that existed at the time was superficial and merely temporary. Yet I think not. Joe Clark and I arranged a student exchange between his home town of High River, Alberta, and my riding. While this was a small initiative, it was symbolic. I had great hope.

Diefenbaker's antipathy towards the two-nations gambit came as no surprise to me. In the late fall of 1966, I had made a speech at McMaster University in Hamilton. During a press interview, a reporter asked me what I thought about my leader's continued references to "one Canada." I answered that I appreciated Diefenbaker's sentiments in this regard and the his firm attitude had obvious merits. I had one qualification, namely, that many French-speaking Canadians, perhaps erroneously, felt that my leader's strong "one Canada" stand possibly endangered the "French fact."

Little did I realize that my gratuitous qualification would plunge me deep into hot water.

The day after my Hamilton visit, I returned to my Ottawa office. Diefenbaker had obviously read the press comments about my interview. One report read, "Grafftey assails Diefenbaker's 'one Canada' stand." Not long after my arrival, the phone rang and I was called immediately to the leader's office. Soon I was confronted by an enraged lion, out of control, shaking and waving his finger at me. "By the Gauls," he screamed. "What nonsense! I never expected such an outrage from you, Grafftey. Haven't you read your history? I stand firmly with Sir John A." On "One Canada," Dief had lost his temper. He was in orbit. At one point, he picked up an ashtray, and I was not entirely convinced he wasn't about to throw it at me. When I attempted to reply, he merely got up, went to the door, and opened it with by a loud "Get out." Mike Starr, who had served with such distinction as Labour minister, was sitting in the waiting room to see the Chief. In a later conversation, he told me he nearly entered the office during the visit, as he honestly thought violence was about to break out.

The history of the thirty years speaks for itself. The results are there for all to see.

In the summer of 1935 in Sherbrooke, Quebec, Maurice Duplessis, together with a group of dissident Liberals and Conservatives, founded the Union Nationale party. In less than two years, the Liberals left the party, leaving the UN as a Conservative force, largely resented in rural and small-town Québec. After Duplessis' death in January 1959, Paul Sauvé took over as premier only to die in office less than a year later. Within a year Jean Lesage became premier, in the spring of 1960. After him, Daniel Johnson, by the strength of incredibly hard work and Lesage's arrogance, would become premier in 1966. He, too, died suddenly in office in 1968, to be succeeded by Jean-Jacques Bertrand, who would be defeated in the spring of 1970 by Robert Bourassa. Bertrand died soon thereafter, leaving the Union Nationale in total disarray. In a little over ten years, four leaders of the UN had died, three of them suddenly. The vacuum would soon be filled by extreme nationalist and separatist elements that would spur on the Parti Québécois and René Lévesque. This was the time for the creation of a provincial Progressive Conservative party in the province of Québec. Stanfield, at best, was luke-warm to the idea while Mulroney and his coterie of Montréal organizers opposed it outrightly. A provincial Conservative party could have occupied a middle ground between René Lévesque's separatist movement and the uncompromising centralist views of Pierre Trudeau.

Trudeau detested Maurice Duplessis and he had few good words for Lester Pearson's ideas about cooperative federalism. His strong socialist views supported an equally strong federal authority, which left little room for provincial rights. We were in for a prolonged period of province-bashing, together with confrontation of Québec and its leaders.

The years 1968 to 1972 could and should have been years for rebuilding the PC party in Québec from the grass roots. They were not. I find this hard to understand. Stanfield had taken over the Nova Scotia Tories when they held no seats in that province, as did Peter Lougheed in Alberta, who found himself, as leader, in the same position. Stanfield had experience in building from the bottom up. Maybe Québec political organization seemed incomprehensible to him, as it had to his predecessors as leader. Once more in 1972, on the advice of Mulroney and others, Stanfield embraced the lietenancy theory. Claude Wagner, a Liberal attorney general in the Lesage government and subsequently a provincial court judge, was drafted at the very last moment as Québec lieutenant. Wagner came at a high price. The party had to set up a $300,000 trust fund in order to convert the judge to the Conservative cause. This whole operation shocked and disillusioned rural Québec voters who, under proper circumstances, would have supported PC candidates. In 1972, Stanfield came within a seat of defeating the Liberals — but elected only two members in Québec: Wagner and myself.

At a time when Trudeau was simultaneously alienating the West and confronting Québec separatism, my party had opted out of any serious activity in the province of Québec. Trudeau's secretary of state, Gérard Pelletier, putting his country before party, often warned Trudeau about the ultimate consequences of his politics of confrontation, but to no avail. The constitutional debate had become politicized between the extremes of Trudeau's confrontation and separatism. Having opted out of meaningful political activity and the constitutional debate up to 1979 in my province, my party has to shoulder part of the blame for the current state of affairs.

Joe Clark, as prime minister, attempted to occupy the constitutional middle ground. He talked about a "community of communities." I never began to understand what he meant. I doubt if he did either.

The 1980 referendum in Québec left me with a distinct feeling of unease. It was in many ways more like an election campaign than a referendum. Federal and provincial Liberals were pitted against the Parti Québécois. My party was totally marginalized in the debate, even though most members would vote *non* to sovereignty. I was invited by senior Liberal organizers in my riding to speak for the federal cause, which I did. It always seemed to me that constitutional debate should not be the stuff of partisan politics. The referendum was an exercise in extreme partisanship.

Before 1983, Clark was too preoccupied with defending his leadership to build up the party in Québec. In 1983, Mulroney took over. Building from the grass roots up was not his bag. After the referendum, provincial and federal Liberals were at loggerheads, and in no time, Mulroney and Bourassa would strike up an alliance. Mulroney would go on to strike up a similar alliance with the PQ and the most extreme nationalist and separatist elements in the province. He came to power with a grab bag of members from Québec, members whose allegiance to separatism far exceeded their loyalty to Canada. Lucien Bouchard is only one case in point. By such short-term expediency, Mulroney gave up one of the most important traditional powers Canadian prime ministers have had — the power to define and defend the federal cause. Over the years, he has sounded more like a chairman speaking for provincial premiers than a champion for Canada and the federal authority. Two election victories are all well and good, but Mulroney's ability to lead constitutional renewal — such as it was — has been compromised and damaged beyond repair. Nothing more clearly symbolizes the breakdown of the federal authority and "politics as usual" than the rise of the Reform Party in the West — and the Bloc Québécois in Québec. Among other things, renewed federal leadership must marry Québec nationalism with the valid aspirations of Western Canada. This will go a long way towards uniting Canada and giving us a new constitution.

Britain had its constitution, largely unwritten, and every schoolchild in the United States knows something about theirs. A constitution is the very foundation of a country, its government, and the basic framework from which most laws emanate. This should also be true for Canada, but unfortunately, our constitutional history symbolized our national uncertainty and division. Constitutions are political documents in the truest and broadest sense of the word. Constitutions and the political will they are founded upon are meant to reflect national stability. Judging by these criteria, we must see that Canada is currently in terrible shape. So much of what is wrong with our practices at all levels of government stems from constitutional confusion and instability. We can and should do better, but those who speak out for constitutional change and reform will have to be more precise in what they mean. For well over thirty years, the constitutional debate has gone on between politicians and bureaucrats. The people have been left out of the discussions. They have been left confused by slogans put together behind closed doors. Who knows what they mean — "Two Nations," "Special Status," "Cooperative Federalism," "Community of Communities," "*Maîtres chez nous*," "Sovereignty Association," Separation," "Equality or Independence," "Notwithstanding Clause," "Parallel Agreement," "Opting Out," "Distinct Society." The so-called constitutional experts have had a field day, and the list seems never-ending. Just recently I was at a symposium on national unity at McGill University. For the first time I heard the expression "Asymmetrical Federalism." It was based on the notion that sovereignty association could be the result of some new kind of federalism. Since nobody at the symposium knew what sovereignty association meant, it is not hard to imagine that my request for a clarification of the concept "Asymmetrical Federalism" was met with prolonged and stony silence among the academic and resident constitutional experts. Lack of precision in constitutional debate leaves the door open for political demagogues.

In order to effect meaningful constitutional change, attitudes must change. Irrespective of our individual persuasions, we must stamp out intolerance, bigotry, the rise of racism, and politicians who pit English against French for votes.

English-speaking Canadians will have to show willingness to question the current relevance and utility of many institutions and practices we have heretofore cherished and considered indispensable. They will seriously have to consider the immediate abolition of the monarchy, to be replaced by a Canadian head of state, the abolition of the Senate, and the possible creation of a presidential system of government based on separation of powers. French-speaking Canadians will have to realize that as long as Québec Bill 178 (the Québec language law) stands as is on the statute books, no Canadian enjoys "freedom of speech." Those who say the notion of collective rights is more important to francophones than that of individual rights are doing a disservice to Canada and to French-speaking Canadians, who can be counted on for fairness, decency, and civility. The present language law has been imposed on them in a mean-spirited atmosphere of demagoguery by an élitist few, out of touch with the people. To compound the felony, federal leadership has ceased in Ottawa. The Québec government must realize federalism is a two-way street. Mr. Bourassa cannot have his cake and eat it too.

There will be no separation. French-speaking and English-speaking Canadians have grown to love Canada. When I think of 1867, I think of a marriage, a political marriage of sacramental significance, an act of faith. While we have become a somewhat secular society, Canadians avoid divorce when possible.

When I was fifteen years old and in high school, I was unavoidably absent from physics classes when magnetism and electricity were taught. I didn't have the good sense to ask for extra coaching, so I have never understood the basics of this particular discipline. Consequently, in subsequent physics exams, both in high school and in college, I could write only for 80 per cent of the total marks, as electricity and magnetism normally counted for 20 per cent of the total.

When I started out in politics, the Progressive Conservative Party reminded me of my problem with physics. In any general election, Québec was normally written off as a lost cause. The Tory party would only go for seventy of the seats, naming Québec candidates at the very last moment. The party did not put down its roots in Québec at the grass-roots level. It still has not. Mulroney's Québec majorities were based on ill-conceived expediency and "unholy alliances." The country is paying a heavy price now. The party will pay an even greater price later.

Had the Progressive Conservative Party roots in Québec, surely its voice from that province could have constituted a moderate option for constitutional reform, as opposed to the rigid polarization we have today. Québec and western nationalism could have become a unifying force for the good of Canada. Instead, we have Mulroney's ex-friend, Lucien Bouchard, leading the Bloc Québécois in Québec, and another very close friend, Richard Holden, a member of the English Rights Equality Party in the same province. Simultaneously, we have seen the rise of the Reform Party under Preston Manning. The emergence of these regional parties underlines the total bankruptcy of the Mulroney constitutional approach.

The U.S. president Harry Truman once said, " A leader has to lead, otherwise he has no business in politics." We may ask ourselves, Where is that leadership today? Who is speaking for Canada?

To preserve the union, we must have leadership in Ottawa, leadership that defines and defends the federal cause. Macdonald and Cartier, working with the provinces, were just such leaders, as were most of our successive prime ministers.

In order to effect constitutional renewal, Canadians and legislative authorities must be consulted over a long period of time. Broad and meaningful consultation will be the order of the day before an "Estates Général" or "Constitutional Convention" puts the finishing touches on "A New and Modern Constitution."

This process of national renewal will bring Canadians under the framework of a new and modern constitution suited to modern times. Macdonald and Cartier would be the first to wish us well. They would be the first to congratulate us once this act of statesmanship is completed — statesmanship that will, in the very best sense, "*trust the people.*"

14

MORE UNFINISHED BUSINESS

The Liberal convention that chose Jean Chrétien was just more of the same. Ross Howard of *The Globe and Mail* Ottawa bureau wrote on February 16, 1990: "Five Liberal leadership candidates, before the 1990 spring convention, spent an estimated $7 million — dollars by and large raised in central Canada. This was done when the party itself was over $4 million in debt. The candidates did not have to disclose who donated how much. Chrétien and Paul Martin each spent up to the spending limits of $1.7 million, while Sheila Copps, the so-called populist candidate, spent about $1 million. So much for democracy!"

The same kind of Tory caucus revolt that brought down Edward Heath and put Margaret Thatcher at the head of the British Tory Pary has now evicted the "Iron Lady" from Number 10 Downing Street. What about Canada? How do we get rid of a prime minister in mid-term? How do we evict him from 24 Sussex Drive? Are we meant just to sit by, to wonder and hope for the best? Are we about to go into another federal election with a crop of national leaders named by an outmoded and archaic system?

Let's hope not. Let's hope to see a new slate of leaders — elected openly by the rank and file of their respective parties, giving one vote each to duly accredited party members.

Party Candidates

There is no magic formula to guarantee that party candidates are chosen freely at the grass-roots level. Eternal vigilance by a concerned citizenry, collectively and individually, provides the only assurance that candidates will be named and put forward in a truly democratic manner. A bona fide nominating convention must be called, with proper notice given by the party executive. The party executive, as we have seen, must have been named by the membership "at large," under the terms of a constitution drafted and approved by the same membership. If we fail to carry out our responsibilities in this regard, things will go on in the same old way — and the "voice of the people" will rarely be heard in the Commons. Party leaders, together with the hierarchy in Ottawa, will, in most cases, continue to control local constituency nominations. It is my belief that, currently, in North America, we are witnessing a healthy degree of local self-initiative, involving many of the positive aspects of legitimate "populism." If this contention turns out to be true, it will be so only because each of us takes seriously his or her community responsibilities.

Budget-making and the Bureaucracy

No longer can we permit government to be seriously crippled by letting the Finance department operate in almost total secrecy. We have seen that, since 1957, every government and its Finance minister have, on at least one occasion, been gravely wounded as the result of Finance measures, such as the GST or budgets that have been drafted in secrecy without any real political control. If Parliament is to regain control of the purse strings, budget-making must be brought out of the closet into the open.

The bureaucracy in Canada is yet another question. Compared to bureaucrats the world over, I do not believe that, at any given time, our public servants are politically partisan. That is not the problem. The problem us that they tend to become a law unto themselves, especially when it comes to the formulation of policy. Our elected representatives, by and large, have avoided their responsibilities in the policy area, and public servants rush with glee into the vacuum.

Public servants abhor advice from outside their ranks, advice that is often tendered by the private sector. More and more, ministers act as rubber stamps, while big decisions are made by a select group of non-elected insiders within the Prime Minister's Office and the upper reaches of the public service. As well, Mulroney's style of management has become top heavy. He has increased the role his own advisers play in the decisions that go to cabinet. Everything has to touch the "royal jelly." We now have an inner cabinet, a planning and priorities committee, and a smaller inner-inner cabinet — an informal eight-member operations committee known as "ops." This cabinet committee now does what the Planning and Priorities Committee used to do — set the cabinet agenda and decide how to spend tax dollars.

In 1940, Louis St. Laurent had eighteen cabinet ministers; Pierre Trudeau had twenty-four; in 1979, Joe Clark had a thirty-member cabinet. Mulroney's cabinet of forty is obviously too big to be effective, especially when we consider that, in the United States, the presidential cabinet at the White House normally numbers about twelve. Most cabinet ministers today are marginal to the real decision-making process. They are shifted far too often, leaving before they have a real grip on their respective departments. Dr. Robert Jackson, a professor of political science at Carleton University, stated,

"Cabinet has become more a symbolic institution to satisfy the needs of regional representation and special interests."

The fundamental issue of legitimate political control of the bureaucracy must be faced the moment a new government takes over and the cabinet is sworn in. In my active political lifetime in Canada, since 1957, no government has come to office with a comprehensive political or policy agenda. Whether we like it or not, Ronald Reagan and Margaret Thatcher came to office with clear neo-conservative policy initiatives. Who, of my generation, can ever forget Franklin Roosevelt and his liberal New Deal agenda. If it is true to say that the era of competing ideologies is over, that does not absolve political leaders from formulating and communicating comprehensive policies based on "party" principles or doctrine, as the case may be. The public can and must demand no less.

By failing to fulfil this obvious requirement, successive Canadian governments have left the "policy" agenda largely in the hands of permanent public servants.

In the case of the present government in Ottawa, we have seen some major individual initiatives — notably free trade, Meech Lake, and the GST. Important as they are, they should not, in any way, be confused with a comprehensive, well-integrated, policy agenda that has captured the public's imagination. Successive governments and their leaders have been so preoccupied with "politicking as usual" that they have come to power with no new ideas or clear directions. While modern-day demands for getting elected are understandable, we should ask the question "Getting elected to do what?" When governments come to power without a policy agenda, we merely get government by "ad hockery," which merely responding to events as they come up. Under such circumstances, when political leaders abandon their responsibilities, permanent officials more quickly into the policy arena, and "responsible" government suffers. Since the middle of the twentieth century this has too often been the case in Canada.

ACCESS AND THE DRIP-DOWN THEORY

Access

Most members of Parliament know what "access" means. Soon after their election, they must prepare themselves to receive their constituents on a regular basis. I had my "clinics" in Knowlton every weekend when I returned from Ottawa. First of all, I set up my constituency office in a spare room of my home. When the government authorized funds for constituency offices, I rented an office in the village, to be run and organized by my constituency staff. Later on, I would travel to various towns on Saturdays, and the mayors would lend me their offices to receive constituents, who were often without the means to travel any distance to meet me. My constituents would contact me by visit, mail, or phone. The phone never stopped ringing, and my mail boxes in Knowlton and Ottawa were always full. Constituents also had "access" to me when I attended events in their towns.

I soon became known as a pen thief. When I visited individual homes or attended functions, I would keep pen and paper in my pocket to take notes when anybody came up to me with a request. Often, the individual in question would hand me a pen to facilitate the operation. When I arrived home, usually around midnight, I would empty my pockets on my desk and arrange the notes. Unfortunately, with the notes were usually to be found a good number of pens I simply had not returned to their owners. Keeping in touch and giving complete access to my electors was a must for me if public service was to mean anything at all. In a riding such as mine, social agencies that we invariably find in larger urban areas simply do not exist. Constituents depend on their "member" for help that often does not strictly fall under his or her defined federal responsibilities. In low-income, small-town, and rural areas, individual citizens must have "access" to their member. It seems to me that "access" should be the watchword for legislators in a free and democratic society.

Once I was in Ottawa, it became apparent to me that some of the basic principles of "access" were compromised. Those most in need simply cannot travel to the nation's capital. Senators scurry around the corridors of power, often acting as *ex officio* lobbyists for what Diefenbaker used to call "the powerful."

Party fund-raising has everything to do with access. When parties and their leadership candidates raise millions of unreported dollars, questions must be asked. At fund-raising dinners for my party, there is usually a reception for a select few "friends of the party" before the dinner itself. The select few must give a minimum of $1,000 annually in order to get in the door for the pre-dinner ritual. In return, they get to meet the prime minister and cabinet ministers in attendance and to get "their ear." The thousand or so in attendance at the dinner itself must be satisfied with a rousing partisan speech and a quick handshake. People without suits are not welcome.

This state of affairs has been translated into a most unhealthy phenomenon in Ottawa itself, where the "voice of the people" has been systematically silenced. The select so-called prestigious inner cabinets manned by senior ministers are not necessarily bad. What is bad relates to ministers and ministries who have been named to these inner cabinet positions during the past twenty-five years. Finance, International Trade, Corporate Affairs, Industry and Trade are examples of ministers almost always elevated to inner cabinet status. It is at this level that the cabinet agenda and spending priorities are decided upon. Other portfolios — which have what I call a broad "people" orientation — are rarely included in these select inner cabinets. They are, as examples, Labour, Health and Welfare, and Agriculture. Access to the top has been thoughtlessly and systematically denied to the less powerful citizens normally represented by the latter ministries. The "less powerful" rarely give big bucks to the parties. All this has seriously affected policy consideration in Ottawa, where, for the last twenty-five years, "trusting the people" has not been the hallmark of federal initiatives. How else to explain what I call the advent of . . . .

The Drip-Down Theory

The 1980s saw the advent of what is now termed "the neo-conservative revolution." Margaret Thatcher in the United Kingdom; Ronald Reagan in the United States; and our own Brian Mulroney pursued with almost religious fervour this philosophy as they bowed at the altar of "neo-conservatism." Whatever Mulroney's instincts, he had little choice, for in bringing down Joe Clark he relied almost totally on the extreme right wing of his party. In all fairness, this revolution had many good aspects. They included an unwillingness merely to throw dollars at social programs and to encourage big government for big government's sake. The drip-down theory, simply stated, goes this way: encourage excellence (not bad in itself), legislate for the powerful, encourage the successful, preach short-term pain for long-term gain, and sooner or later the benefits from this approach will "drip down" to the masses and elevate their status. The problem is that it just doesn't work. Any reading of history soon demonstrates the total bankruptcy of this aspect of the neo-conservative approach. It simply doesn't take into account individual greed and some of the uncaring characteristics of human nature. It is hard to understand, for neo-conservatives have often, correctly in my view, accused socialists of not accepting that the profit motive is writ large in human nature, as is greed. When taking human nature into account, if socialist doctrine underestimates the constructive power of the profit motive and self-interest, surely the neo-conservative ideology is equally guilty of playing down the destructive power of greed. Truth rarely lies at the extremes. Greed was at the heart of the savings and loan debacle in the United States. By indiscriminate deregulation, Ronald Reagan witnessed the scandalous looting of the less fortunate by the greedy.

In all three countries, short-term pain for long-term gain has fallen squarely on the shoulders of the "less fortunate." This slogan is supportable only when the sacrifice is evenly distributed. No amount of smiling rhetoric can hide the evil results of the drip-down theory in action. We can only be encouraged at some signals that point to the end of the neo-conservative revolution in all three countries and to the beginning of new and "caring" societies in the 1990s.

Edmund Burke's famous letter to his electors has often been cited and quoted. He tells us, with reason, that an elected public official in a free and democratic society can never be just a rubber stamp for public opinion on any given issue at any given time. Character and leadership demand more than from our elected officials. Leadership by "opinion polls" is no leadership at all. Leadership is obviously a fundamental requirement for democratic survival. "Trusting the people" does not mean "governing by the polls." Trusting the people will not open up the floodgates of mindless, populist anarchy. To trust the people means to communicate openly and to consult meaningfully with them. Trusting the people means the end to all the undemocratic notions of paternalism and elitism that so often plague our governing bodies.

In late August 1965, the Progressive Conservative Party held a policy forum at Fredericton, New Brunswick. Marshall McLuhan addressed the participants. "The medium," he said, was "the message." I felt, instinctively, he was saying something relevant and important. But, in all honesty, I didn't know what it was all about. I really didn't understand him. It was like hearing modern poetry, looking at modern art, or listening to some contemporary music for the very first time. Everybody feigned interest. Nobody really understood or appreciated. Twenty-six years later, I am beginning to understand and appreciate.

It is loosely stated that "the process killed Meech Lake; the process savaged the GST." What all this really means is that policies and initiatives that are not properly explained or communicated to the public are doomed to failure. We might say that it has always been thus in democratic societies. But in a day and age of instant communications, the need to explain clearly and properly becomes imperative. The media and communications assume the importance of substance. Substance and communications are one and the same. The media are the message. The surgeon at the operating table and the mechanic at the garage really do not have to communicate in the truest sense in order to successfully conclude their work. The politician and statesman must. To say that Winston Churchill could not have been packaged for the requirements of modern-day communications is irrelevant.

"The medium is the message" means, among other things, that leaders in democratic societies will have to recognize that "explanation and communication" are in fact, substance. Elitism will suffer. Democracy and freedom will be well served for, going into a new century, politicians and statesmen will have to "*trust the people.*"

INDEX

Abbott, Doug, 22–23, 129, 134
Abbott, John Joseph Caldwell, 40
access, 203–205
advertising, campaign, 97
advisers, 136, 137, 143, 144, 146, 166; *See also* officials, non-elected; public servants/service
agrarianism, Western, 74
Agriculture, Department/Minister of, 205
Allen, H. C., 125
al-Mashat, Mohamed, 162
American political practices. *See* under U.S.
anarchy, 206
André, Harvie, 107
anglophones. *See* English-speaking Canadians/Quebeckers
annuities, deferred, 142
"anybody-but-Clark" strategy, 104, 109
apathy, 3, 4, 5
Archambault, Maurice, 20, 26, 27
Argue, Hazen, 51–52
assistant deputy ministers, 135
association, party, 25
"asymmetrical federalism," 195
Attlee, Clement, 127
auditors general, 125
audits, 114, 116

background papers, 145
Baker, Walter, 103, 168
balance-of-payments deficit, 133
Balcer, Léon, 21, 22, 27
ballots, 43–44, 47, 48
Bank of Canada, 128, 128–129, 132, 135, 156–161
bank collapses, 124
Bégin, Joseph D., 17–18
Beattie Brothers Farm Equipment, 15
Bennett, R. B., 49
Benson, Edgar, 143
Bertrand, Gabrielle (Mrs. Jean-Jacques), 9, 32–33
Bertrand, Jean-François, 187–188
Bertrand, Jean-Jacques, 16, 19, 20, 26, 187, 192
"big government," 205
bigotry, 195
Bill 178 (Québec language law), 196
Bill C-114, 158, 160
Black, Eldon, 180
Blaikie, Peter, 105
Blake, Edward, 42, 43
Blenkarn, Don, 123
Bloc Québécois, 171, 194, 197

"blow-in delegate," 5
blue-collar workers, 78
Borden, Robert, 43–44, 45, 46, 48
Bouchard, Lucien, 92, 171, 194, 197
Bourassa, Robert, 192, 194, 196
Bourbonnais, Marcel, 131
Bowell, Mackenzie, 40–41
Boyer, J. Patrick, 28
Bracken, John, 90
Bradford, Bob, 59
The Breakers Inn, 173
briefings/briefing papers, 167, 170–171
Britain, 194, 202; political practices in, 1, 37, 38–39, 41, 42, 53, 54, 66–69, 111, 124, 125–126, 127–128, 139
British North America (BNA) Act, 129–130
Broadbent, Ed, 53
Brome County (Que.), 14, 15–19, 21–22
Brome–Missisquoi (Que.) riding, 4, 5, 6–9, 13, 19–23, 25–27, 32–33, 108, 153
Brown, George, 37, 38, 41
Brown, Glen, 19
Brown, Rosemary, 53
Bryce, Bob, 126–127
budget debates, 137, 171
budgets: control over preparing, 137, 141, 143–147, 200–201; importance of, 125; problems with, 128–129, 136–147
budget scheduling, 145
budget secrecy, 101, 123, 126, 126–128, 140, 141, 143–147, 200–203
budget speeches, 132, 137, 144
bureaucracy/bureaucrats. *See* public servants/service
Burke, Edmund, 206
Burns, James, 146
Bush, George, 176
busing, 2, 30
Butler, Esmond, 175

cabinet: appointments to, 111, 151–152, 163–164, 173–176; and Finance department, 132, 134, 143; full, 140, 147, 182; inner, 182, 201, 204–205; inner-inner, 201, 204–205; and leadership selection, 43–44, 110, 138; and non-elected officials, 124, 201; size/role of, 201–202; in U.S., 201
cabinet agenda, 201, 204–205
cabinet committees, 124, 168, 169, 182, 201
cabinet documents, 140, 170–171
cabinet meetings, 124, 168, 169, 170, 173
cabinet ministers: and budgets/budget secrecy, 127, 136–138, 142–143;

208

INDEX

duties/role of, 140–141, 165–166, 179, 201; and legislation, 123; and ministers of state, 166; and parliamentary committees, 135, 155, 156; and public servants/service, 137, 166, 167, 168, 169, 170; relations among, 180; shifting of, 174–175, 178–179, 201; *See also* ministerial responsibility; ministers of state
cabinet secrecy, 169, 170
cabinet shuffles, 174–175, 178–179, 201
cabinet spending priorities, 201, 204–205
Cameron, Stevie, 28
campaign management, 25
Camp, Dalton, 20, 74, 75, 76, 79
Canada Elections Act, 84, 114, 115–116
Canada Pension Plan, 166, 189
Canadian Broadcasting Corporation (CBC), 152
Canadianization of industries, 128
Canadian Tax Foundation, 144–145
Canadian Transport Commission, 152
candidate nomination, 14, 15, 17–23, 25–32, 33, 38, 54–66, 110–111, 200
Caouette, Réal, 134–135, 139
capital-gains tax, 141
Carter, James Earl ("Jimmy"), 64
Cartier, Sir George-Etienne, 187, 188, 197, 198
caucuses, party: in Britain, 66–67, 68, 199; and confidence motions, 138, 139–140; and economic policy, 123, 124, 134, 147; and leadership selection, 39, 40–44, 46, 47, 48, 92, 104, 106–107, 110; in U.S., 54–55, 62–63, 65, 72
caucus secrecy, 169
Ceausescu, Nicolae, 72
centralism, 192
Charbonneau, Guy, 98
chiefs of staff, 165–166, 169–170
child tax credit, 167–168
Chirac, Jacques, 69
Chrétien, Jean, 2, 6, 112, 199
Churchill, Gordon, 139–140
Churchill, Winston, 127–128, 207
civil servants/service. *See* public servants/service
Clark, Joe, 89, 98–99, 124, 193–194; named party leader, 6, 7, 79–88, 112; 1979 minority government under, 97–104, 141, 163–183, 201; 1979 fall of government under, 100–104, 105, 107, 128, 140–141, 142; 1980 election loss, 104, 140; defeat as party leader, 104–109; and Mulroney, 92, 96–97, 205; and Québec, 93, 97–99, 163, 164, 190, 193
Cogger, Michel, 7, 33
Coldwell, M. J., 50–51

collective rights, 196
committees: advisory, 144; cabinet, 124, 168, 169, 182, 201; parliamentary, 123, 135, 138, 144, 146, 154–156
communication, of policy decisions/initiatives, 207
Communist Party (PCF), French, 70, 71–72
"community of communities," 193, 195
Compton (Que.), 19
Confederation, 28, 129–131, 187, 188–189, 196
confidence motions/votes, 138–140; *See also* non-confidence votes
confidentiality, 168–169; *See also* secrecy
confrontation, politics of, 190, 192, 193
conscription, 45–46
Conservative party (Britain), 66–67
Conservative Party (Canada), 37, 38, 39–42, 43–44, 48–49, 191; renamed Progessive Conservatives, 90
Conservatives, Independent, 139
constituency conventions, 15–23, 25–26, 27, 29–31, 32–33, 200
constituents, and access, 203–205
constitution: British, 194; Canadian, 138, 194–195; U.S., 194
constitutional conferences/conventions, 188, 189, 197
constitutional issues, 93, 187–198
consultation, by Finance ministers, 141, 143–146, 147
contributions, 114–116; and access, 204–205; defining, 115; limits on, 115; *See also* funding, campaign
conventions. *See* constituency conventions; constitutional conferences/conventions; leadership conventions; leadership-review conventions; nominating conventions; party conventions; policy conferences/conventions
Co-operative Commonwealth Federation (CCF), 49–51; *See also* New Democratic Party (NDP)
cooperative federalism, 192, 195
Co-operative Movement, 142
Copps, Sheila, 199
Corporate Affairs, Department/Minister of, 204
corporations, 114, 117, 180
correspondence, parliamentary, 177
Cournoyer, Louis, 6, 7, 8–9, 26, 27
Coutts, Jim, 27
Cowansville (Que.), 7–9, 26–27, 27, 33, 131–132
Coyne, James, 128, 156–161
Créditistes, 134–135, 139
credit squeeze, 134
Crombie, David, 166, 167
Crosbie, John, 101, 108, 128, 141, 143, 144

cross-voting, 114
Cuban Missile Crisis, 169
currency devaluation, 126–127, 128, 132–134, 139

Dalton, Hugh, 127–128
Daughters of Liberty, 126
Defence, Department/Minister of National, 155, 169
deferred annuities, 142
deficits, campaign, 96
de Gaulle, Charles, 70
delegates: at large, 5, 63; "blow-in," 5, 78, 85; ex officio, 5, 53, 78, 79, 85
delegate registration, 5, 107
delegate selection, 2, 6–9, 18, 26, 47–48, 52, 63, 73, 77–78, 84–85, 88, 104, 108–109, 112–113; in U.S., 55, 56, 57, 59–63
delegate tracking, 84, 86, 87
demagogues, political, 195
democracy, 24, 161, 204, 206, 207; and budget/GST secrecy, 123, 124; and candidate nomination, 14, 15, 23, 26, 27, 28–32, 33, 55, 5758, 65, 200; and leadership selection, 1–4, 9, 14, 15, 18, 49, 52–53, 67, 69, 79, 87, 104, 109, 110–120, 199–200; and taxation, 123–135
Democratic conventions (U.S.), 44, 57
Denton, Timothy, 146
deputy ministers, 134, 136, 141, 151–152, 164, 166, 167, 168, 171, 176, 180; See also public servants/service
deputy ministers, assistant, 135; See also public servants/service
deputy prime minister, 138
deregulation, 206
Derrick, Brian, 101, 165, 166, 173, 175
devaluation, currency, 126–127, 128, 132–134, 139
developers, 142
Dewey, Tom, 58
Diefenbaker, John ("The Chief"), 24, 79, 89, 90, 129, 131, 141, 172, 182, 189, 190–191, 240; and 1958 election, 102–103, 151–162; and 1962 election, 126, 128, 131–135; and 1968 non-confidence vote, 139; and 1976 leadership convention, 82, 84; 1979 death/funeral of, 172, 173; and bilingualism/biculturalism, 189, 190–191; and candidate nomination, 30–31; debates over leadership by, 74–75, 90, 97; and economic issues, 124, 126–127, 128, 129, 131–135, 156–161; government by/under, 100, 166, 169, 189; selection as party leader, 4–5, 14, 73
Diefenbaker, Olive, 172
Diefendollars, 133

Dirksen, Everett, 58
"distinct society," 195
"divine right to rule" disease, 139
Don Valley East (Ont.) riding, 108–109
Douglas, T. C., 51–52, 138
Doyle, John, 139
Drapeau, Jean, 20
Drew, George, 4, 19, 20, 90
drip-down theory, the, 205–206
Drury, Bud, 151–152
Dulles, John Foster, 58
Dunt, Justin, 64
Duplessis, Maurice, 15, 178–18, 191, 192

Economic Council of Canada, 174
economic policy/issues, 123, 124, 134, 147; See also Finance, Department/Minister of
Economic and Social Affairs committee, 182
Eggleton, Art, 28
Eisenhower, Dwight, 58, 59, 60–62
Election Canada, 116
elections, general: 1945, 23; 1953, 20; 1957, 19–23; 1958, 102–103, 151–162; 1962, 126, 128, 131–135, 139; 1968, 190; 1972, 193; 1979, 97, 164; 1980, 104, 140–141; 1984, 151
elections, primary. See primary elections
Elections Act. See Canada Elections Act
élites, party: and leadership selection, 38–39, 51, 52–53, 55, 78, 81, 82, 85, 88; in Britain, 66, 72, 111; in France, 66, 70–71, 72; in U.S., 55, 57
elitism, 206, 207
"en bloc," registration of delegates, 107
Energy, Mines, and Resources, Department/Minister of, 182–183
energy policy, 100, 101
English Rights Equality Party, 171, 197
English-speaking Canadians/Quebeckers, 187, 188, 190, 195–196
"equality or independence," 195
Equality Party, English Rights, 171, 197
"Estates Généraux," 189, 197
Estimates Committee, 154–155
Etobicoke–Lakeshore (Ont.) riding, 28
exchange rate, foreign, 132–134
excise tax, 141
executive, party, 200
executive assistants, 165–166, 177
expenditure management system, 144
External Affairs, Department/Minister of, 128, 180

Fairweather, Gordon, 76
Faribeault, Maurice, 27–28, 190
farmers, 141, 142
Farnham, 26
Fathers of Confederation, 187, 188–189

INDEX

federalism, 93, 192, 193, 194, 195, 196, 197
Fennell, Scott, 107
Fielding, W. S., 46, 47
Fifth Republic (France), 70, 71
filibusters, 129, 139, 140
Finance, Department/Minister of, 123, 124, 125, 126–127, 128, 129, 131, 132–135, 136–147, 168, 169, 180, 200–203, 204; *See also* National Revenue, Department/Minister of; Revenue Canada
Finance Committee, Commons, 123
fiscal policy, 123–135, 128, 157–158, 161
Fisher, Doug, 136
Fisher, Sidney, 16, 19
fixed rate of exchange, 131–134
Fleming, Donald, 5, 75, 128, 129, 132–134, 143, 157–158, 159
floating rate of exchange, 133
Foot, Michael, 68
Ford, Gerald, 64, 65
foreign capital, 133, 137
foreign exchange rate, 132–134
Forsey, Eugene, 138
Fortin, Luc, 7
Foster, George, 43
Fox, Warwick, 15
francophones, 189, 190; *See also* French-speaking Canadians/ Quebeckers
Fraser, John, 24, 79
Fredericton (NB), 207
freedom of speech, 189, 196
free trade, 202
"French fact," the, 190
French political practices, 66, 69–72
French-speaking Canadians/Quebeckers, 187–188, 195, 196; *See also* francophones
front-runner advantage, 66
Fulton, E. Davie, 5, 75, 79, 89
funding, campaign, 2, 7, 29, 52–53, 78–84, 87, 96, 104, 114–116, 199; in U.S., 56, 64–66
funding, research and development, 181–182
fund-raising, 115, 204

Gamelin (Que.) riding, 28
gasoline tax, 100, 101, 102, 128, 135, 141
Gillies, James, 86, 166
"ginger group," the, 50
Giroux, Fernand, 26
Giscard d'Estaing, Valéry, 70
Globe, 44
Goldwater, Barry, 63
Gordon, Walter, 128, 133, 136–137, 143, 171
governor general, and leadership selection, 38–41, 42, 43–44, 110
Graham, G. P., 46

greed, 205, 206
green papers, 145
Grosart, Alistair, 25–26
GST (Goods and Services Tax), 123, 135, 147, 200, 202, 207
Guarnieri, Albina, 28
Guthrie, Hugh, 49

Hamilton, Alvin, 75, 89, 91
Harkness, Douglas, 169
Harrington Lake, 134
Harris, Walter, 124
head of state, 196
Health and Welfare, Department/Minister of, 164, 166, 182, 205
Heath, Edward, 67, 199
Hees, George, 75
Hellyer, Paul, 79, 82, 85
Higgins Beach (Maine), 173
High River (Alta.), 164, 165, 174, 190
Holden, Richard, 171, 197
Horner, Jack, 79, 82, 83, 87, 93
Howard, Ross, 199
Hudon, Denis, 176, 178
Humphrey, Hubert, 57
Huntington, Ron, 107
Hussein, Saddam, 162

"idiot cards," 178
imported goods, 133
income tax, personal, 138–140
Independent Conservatives, 139
individual rights, 196
Industry and Trade, Department/Minister of, 204
inner cabinet, 182, 201, 204–205
inner-inner cabinet, 201, 204–205
insurance industry, 128, 142
interest rates, 134, 135
International Monetary Fund, 132
International Trade, Department/Minister of, 204
interpretation, and legislation/regulations, 146, 177–178
intolerance, 195
Iran hostage question, 180–181
Iraq, 162
"Iron Lady". *See* Thatcher, Margaret
Iron Ore Company of Canada, 105, 108

Jackson, Robert, 201–202
Johnson, Daniel, 16, 19, 20, 75, 79, 98, 187, 191–192
Johnson, Lyndon B., 99
Johnson, Pierre-Marc, 187–188
Johnson, William, 29
Joliette (Que.), 163
Jolley, Jim, 15, 17, 18–19
Juneau, Pierre, 152

Kennedy, John F., 136, 176
Kierans, Eric, 137
Kingston (Ont.), 38
King, William Lyon Mackenzie, 6, 46, 47, 130
Kirby, Cam, 80
Kirby, Michael, 152
Kissinger, Henry, 100
Knowles, Stanley, 141, 167
Knowlton (Que.), 156, 163, 203

Laakkonen, Allan, 85
Labour, Department/Minister of, 191, 205
Labour party (Britain), 66–67, 67–68, 127–128
labour. *See* unions
Lalonde, Marc, 89
Langevin, Hector, 39
language law, Québec, 196
LaSalle, Roch, 92, 163
Laski, Harold, 125
Laughton, Rodney, 173
Laurier, Sir Wilfrid, 5, 6, 16, 42–43, 44–45, 44–56, 119
Lawson, Bruce, 166
Laxer, James, 53
Lévésque, René, 93, 192
leader, party, role of, 37–38, 50
leadership: federal, 196, 197; party, in U.S., 57
leadership conventions, CCF/NDP, 49–52, 53; Conservative, 53; first held in Canada, 43, 44, 45–48, 48–49, 119; Liberal, 4, 53, 63, 112–113, 199; problems with, 2, 3, 52–53; Progressive Conservative, 4–5, 6–7, 14, 63, 74, 75, 77, 78–87, 93, 104–105, 106, 107, 109, 112–113; in U.S., 110–111; *See also* U.S., leadership selection in
leadership review, 63, 67, 68
leadership-review conventions, 63
leadership selection: 1850 to 1920, 37–44, 110; 1920 to present, 44–52, 110; problems with, 1–6; recommendations for reforming, 110–120; *See also* candidate nomination; *and under* France; U.S.
legislation, and regulation/interpretation, 146, 177–178
Lesage, Jean, 189, 191, 192
letter books, 177
Lewis, David, 53
Liberal Party (Britain), 68–69
Liberal Party (Canada): and 1965 election, 27; and 1968 election, 190; and 1979 election, 97, 164; and 1984 election, 31; and economic issues, 136–137, 138–140, 141–142; and leadership selection, 2, 4, 5–6, 42–48, 52, 53, 63, 138, 139, 140, 173, 199; provincial, 47,

193, 194; and public servants/service, 151–153; in Québec, 191, 193, 194
lieutenancy principle, 27–28
life-insurance industry, 128, 142
Lodge, Henry Cabot, 61
Longueuil (Que.), 108
Lortie, Jean-Yves, 107
Lougheed, Peter, 80, 81, 101, 192
Lower Canada College, 17
Luce, Clare Booth, 58
Lynseth, Del, 166

MacArthur, Douglas, 58
McCutcheon, Wallace, 75
Macdonald, Donald, 144
MacDonald, Flora, 20, 76, 79, 80, 81, 85, 86, 87, 180, 181
Macdonald, Sir John A., 37, 39, 187, 188, 191, 197, 198
MacDonald, Sandfield, 41–42
MacEachen, Allan, 102, 128, 141–142, 143, 144–145
Macey, Margaret, 164
McGill University, 17
McGovern–Fraser Commission (U.S.), 57–58, 63
McGrath Committee on Parliamentary Reform, 155
Mackasey, Bryce, 177
MacKay, Elmer, 106
Mackenzie, Alexander, 42
McKnight, Bill, 107
McLaughlin, Audrey, 2
McLay, Jeannine, 17
McLuhan, Marshall, 207
McNab, Gordon, 182–183
"*Maîtres chez nous,*" 189, 195
Major, John, 67
mandarins. *See* public servants/service
Manning, Preston, 197
Marchais, Georges, 71–72
Maritime provinces, 131
Martieth, Waldo, 182
Martin, Paul, 5, 138, 199
Martin, W. M., 46
Masse, Marcel, 175–176, 182–183
media, 3, 73–74, 81, 82, 87, 92, 118, 127–128, 168–169, 170, 207
Medicare, 189
"The medium is the message," 207
Meech Lake, 188, 202, 207
Meighen, Arthur, 43–44, 48–49
membership, party, 38, 113–114, 199–200
membership cards, 6–7, 28, 29–30, 112–114
Mercure, Gilles, 33
Michener, Roland, 24
ministerial responsibility, 183
ministers of state, 164, 166–167, 178; *See also* cabinet ministers

INDEX 213

ministry of state for Science and Technology (MOSST), 173, 176, 178
minority governments, 97–104, 138–140, 141, 153, 163–183, 201
Mireault, Gaétan, 22
Missisquoi County (Que.), 16, 20, 22
Mississauga (Ont.), 28
Mitterand, François, 69, 70
monarchy, abolition of, 195–196
Monck, Lord, 39
monetary policy, 157, 158, 161
money bills, defeats on, 136, 138
Montmorency (Que.), 77
Montréal, 7, 28, 32, 90, 91, 97, 104, 131, 190; *See also* Québec
Montreal Lumber Company, 15–16, 17
Montreal Neurological Institute, 181–182
Morgan, Keith, 108
Mount Allison University, 17
Mount Royal Liberal Association, 27
MPs: access to, 203–205; role of, 153–154, 204
Mulroney, Brian, 99, 155, 190, 194, 201, 205; and 1976 leadership race, 79, 80, 81, 83, 85, 86, 87; and 1983 leadership race, 2, 6, 7–9, 99, 104–109, 112, 205; and 1984 election, 151; and candidate nomination, 31, 33; and constitutional reform, 194, 196–197; during Clark years, 92–93, 96–97, 163, 171, 172; early involvement with PCs, 89–90, 91; and fall of Clark government, 100, 104; and public servants/service, 124, 151, 153, 161–162; and Québec, 192, 193–194, 197

Nader, Ralph, 155
National Defence, Department/ Minister of, 155, 169
nationalism, 128, 137, 190, 192, 194, 197
National Research Council (NRC), 174, 178, 179
National Revenue, Department/Minister of, 134, 165, 168; *See also* Finance, Department/Minister of; Revenue Canada
national unity, 195
Natural Sciences and Engineering Research Council (NSERC), 174, 182–183
neo-conservatism, 202, 205–206
New Brunswick, 131
New Deal agenda, 202
New Democratic Party (NDP), 2, 6, 49, 50, 51–52, 63, 136, 139, 167; *See also* Co-operative Commonwealth Federation (CCF)
Newfoundland, 129–131
NIH (Not Invented Here) syndrome, 166, 171

Nixon, Richard M., 58
nominating conventions, 38, 200
nomination. *See* candidate nomination
non-confidence votes, 101, 103–104, 138–140
non-elected officials. *See* officials, non-elected
"notwithstanding clause," 195
Nova Scotia, 131
Nowlan, George, 128, 134, 137, 169
Nowlan, Pat, 79

officials, non-elected, 100, 102; *See also* public servants/service
officials' gallery, 137
"one Canada" doctrine, 190–191
operations committee ("ops"), 201
opinion polls, 77, 206
opposition party, 4–5, 41–44, 138–140, 141
"opting out," 189, 195
organization, party, 25
Ouimet, Alphonse, 152

"A Paper on Budget Secrecy and Proposals for Broader Consultation" (MacEachen), 143, 144–145
"parallel agreement," 195
parliamentary committees. *See* committees, parliamentary
parliamentary secretary, 128, 134, 135, 169
Parti Québécois, 118, 188, 192, 193, 194
party association, 25
party candidates. *See* candidate nomination
party conventions: Conservative, 48–49; first held in Canada, 43, 44; Liberal, 45–48; Progressive Conservative, 104–105, 106, 107; in U.S., 55, 56–57, 65
party executive, 200
party leaders. *See* leadership selection
party organization, 25
paternalism, 206
patronage appointments, 98–99
PCF. *See* Communist Party (PCF), French
Pearkes, George, 155
Pearson, Lester B. ("Mike"), 4, 5–6, 124, 126, 138–140, 151–152, 173, 189, 192
pegging of dollar, 132–134
Pelletier, Gérard, 93, 193
Penfield, Wilder, 181–182
pension policy, 124, 166–167
personal income tax, 138–140
Persons, Eddie, 15, 17, 18, 19
Petro-Canada, 100, 101
Pickersgill, Jack, 152
pipeline debate, 129
Pitfield, Michael, 89, 152
Planning and Priorities committee, 201

214　　　　　　　　　　　　　　　　　　　　　　　　　　　　　　　INDEX

policy: economic, 123–135, 136–147, 157–158, 161, 166–167; energy, 100, 101; and private sector, 127, 180; and public servants/service, 166, 169–170; science, 173, 178, 179, 181–182
policy advisers, 166; *See also* advisers
policy agenda, importance of, 202–203
policy conferences/conventions, 38, 45, 50, 77, 207
policy decisions: communicating to public, 207; responsibility for, 37– 38, 178–179, 180, 201, 202–203, 205
policy forums, 207
policy papers, 145
Political Action Committee (PAC), 64–65
"politics of confrontation," 190, 192, 193
polls, opinion, 77, 206
populism, 200, 206
populist candidate, 199
Port Arthur (Ont.), 136
pre-budget period, 144, 145
presidential system, 94, 96, 111, 153, 196
Price, Maj.-Gen. Basil, 22–23
primary elections: in Britain, 68; in U.S., 54, 55–56, 57, 59, 60, 62–63, 65–66, 72, 110
prime minister, power of, 1, 111, 141, 169, 194
Prime Minister's Office (PMO), 140, 166, 173, 174, 180, 201
Prince Edward Island, 131
prisoners, rehabilitation of, 94
private sector: and budget measures, 142, 143; and policy direction, 127; and public service, 153, 170–171, 179, 180
Privy Council, clerks of, 126–127, 141, 152, 175, 182–183
Privy Council Office (PCO), 140, 166, 169, 180
profit motive, 206
Progressive Conservative Party: and 1953 election, 20; and 1957 election, 19–23; and 1958 election, 102–103, 151–162; and 1962 election, 126, 128, 131–135, 139; and 1965 policy forum, 207; and 1979 fall of government, 100–104, 105, 107, 128, 140–141, 142; and 1980 election, 104, 140–141; and 1984 election, 151; and candidate nomination, 19–23, 26–27, 30–33; and leadership selection, 2, 3, 4–5, 6–9, 14, 53, 63, 73–88; name of (1942), 90–91; in Newfoundland, 129–131; provincial, 192; in Québec, 90–93, 97–98, 134–135, 163, 171, 190, 192–194, 196–197
Progressive Party, 50, 90
provincial rights, 192
public servants/service, 137, 153, 163, 168–169, 180, 195, 201–203; and cabinet, 165–166, 167, 168–171, 175, 179, 180, 182–183; and control of purse strings, 123–135; and Diefenbaker, 151, 152, 156–161, 166; and ministers of state, 166–167, 176–177, 178; and Mulroney, 153, 161–162; and parliamentary committees, 156; and Pearson, 151–152; and policy, 166, 169–170; and private sector, 153, 170–171, 201; and Trudeau, 152; *See also* deputy ministers; Finance, Department/Minister of; officials, non-elected
Public Service Act, 174

Quartering Act, 125
Québécois, 187, 189–190; Bloc, 171, 194, 197; Parti, 118, 188, 192, 193, 194
Québec: and 1980 referendum, 193, 194; and Clark, 98–99, 173; and constitutional crisis, 187–188, 196; Créditistes in, 134–135; and Diefenbaker, 189; language law (Bill 178), 196; and Mulroney, 192, 193–194, 197; nationalism in, 190, 192, 194, 197; premiers of, 191–192; Progressive Conservatives in, 90–93, 97–98, 163, 171, 190, 192–194, 196–197; Quiet Revolution, 189; and sovereignty, 193; and Union Nationale, 191; *See also* Bloc Québécois; English-speaking Canadians/Quebeckers; French-speaking Canadians/Quebeckers; Montréal; Parti Québécois; Québécois; Québec City; Union Nationale
Québec City, 98–99, 129, 173
Queen Elizabeth Hotel (Montréal), 108
Question Period, 178
Quiet Revolution, 189

racism, 195
Radio-Canada, 189
Rae, Bob, 101
Rasminsky, Louis, 160
Rassemblement pour la République (RPR) (France), 69, 70
Reagan, Ronald, 63–66, 202, 205, 206
Red Chamber, the. *See* SenateRed Tories, 79
referendum, Québec (1980), 193, 194
Reform Party, 37, 38, 41–42
Reform Party of Canada, 194, 197
regionalism, 187, 197; *See also* Bouchard, Lucien; English Rights Equality Party; Manning, Preston; Reform Party
regulations, and legislation, 146, 177–178
representation, 52–53, 57
Republican National Committee (U.S.), 58, 60
Republican Party (France), 70

INDEX

Republican party (U.S.), 58–62, 65
research and development, 147, 179, 181–182; *See also* Science and Technology
responsible government, 202–203
Revenue Canada, 116; *See also* Finance, Department/Minister of; National Revenue, Department/Minister of
Rideau Hall, 164, 165, 174, 176
rights, collective vs. individual, 196
Ritz Carlton Hotel (Montréal), 105
Robinson, Jon, 15
Roblin, Duff, 75–77, 78, 79, 109
Rocky Mountain (Alta.) riding, 80
Roosevelt, Franklin D., 202
royal commissions, 130–131
RPR. *See* Rassemblement pour la République (RPR)

St. Antoine–Westmount (Que.) riding, 23
St. Francis Xavier University, 142
St. Jacques (Que.) riding, 108
St. Laurent, Louis Stephen, 5, 6, 19–20, 24, 124, 129, 172–173, 201
Sauvé, Paul, 191
Sauvé, Mrs. Paul, 79
savings and loan crisis, 206
Schneider, Bill, 174, 178
Schreyer, Ed, 175, 176
Science Council of Canada, 174
science policy, 173, 178, 179, 181–182
Science and Technology: Department/Minister of, 123–124, 140, 173–174, 176–183; ministry of state for (MOSST), 173, 176, 178
secrecy: budget, 101, 123, 126, 126–128, 140, 141, 143–147, 200–203; cabinet, 169, 170; caucus, 169; *See also* confidentiality
secretary of state, 193
self-initiative, local, 200
self-interest, 206
Senate, 40, 156, 204; abolition/reform of, 94–96, 196; appointments to, 93–94, 98, 99, 152; U.S., 94, 95
Senate Commerce Committee of Congress (U.S.), 155
separation of powers, 196
separatism, Québec, 93, 192, 193, 194, 196
Sept-Iles (Que.), 108
Sharp, Mitchell, 126, 137, 138, 152
Shaw, Fabie, 22
Sherbrooke (Que.), 191
Silva, Arminde, 28
small-business owners, 141, 142
Smallwood, Joey, 129, 130, 131
Smith, Arthur, 154
Smith, William French, 64
social-credit theory, 135

Social Democratic Party (Britain), 69
socialism, 192, 206
Socialist Party (France), 70–71
Social Programmes, minister of state for, 91, 98, 123–124, 164–165, 166–168
social programs, 124, 205
Sons of Liberty, 126
sovereignty, 193; *See also* constitutional issues; Québec"
"sovereignty association," 195
Spadina (Ont.) riding, 27
Speaking Bureau, Inc., 65
"special status," 195
spending: and cabinet, 201, 204–205; in leadership/election campaigns, 114, 115–116, 199
Speyer, Chris, 106
staff, chiefs of, 165–166, 169–170
Stamp Act, 125–126
Stanfield, Robert: and 1968 non-confidence vote, 138, 139; and 1972 election, 193; and 1976 leadership convention, 84; and constitutional issues, 192–193; and economic issues, 128–129; and leadership selection, 27–28, 74–80, 109, 112; and Mulroney, 90, 92; and Nova Scotia, 192; and Québec, 192–193; and two-nations doctrine, 190
Starr, Michael, 75, 191
The Star, 127
Steel, David, 68
Stevens, Sinclair, 79, 80, 86
subcommittees, 130
suffrage, universal, 113, 117–119
swearing-in procedure, 174–176
Sweetsburg (Que.), 15, 16

Taft, Robert, 58, 59–62
taxes: capital-gains, 141; excise, 141; gasoline, 100, 101, 102, 128, 135, 141; goods and services. *See* GST; personal income, 138–140
Tax Act, 142
taxation without representation, 123–135
tax credit, child, 167–168
tax incentives, 147
tax legislation, 142, 146
tax policy, 123–135, 136–147
tax receipts, and leadership races, 84, 116
tax reform, 142, 144–145
tax specialists, 144
Taylor, Ken, 134, 136, 137, 180–181
Teheran, 181
television, and leadership selection, 73–74
Term 14, 130
Term 29, 129–131
Thatcher, Margaret, 67, 199, 202, 205
Thompson, John, 39–40
Thoms, William, 160–161

throne speeches, 125
Toronto–Greenwood (Ont.) riding, 28
Toronto (Ont.), 38
Trade, Department/Minister of, 138
trade unions. *See* unions
treasury, 133
Treasury Board, 140, 180
Tremblay, Arthur, 98–99
triple-E Senate, 94
Trois-Rivières (Que.), 138
Trudeau, Pierre Elliott, 92, 93, 102, 172, 192, 201, 205; and 1965 election, 27; and 1968 election, 190; and 1979 election, 97, 164; and constitutional issues, 93, 188, 190, 192; and economic issues, 124, 158; and Iran hostage question, 180–181; and leadership selection, 6, 43, 112; and "politics of confrontation," 190, 192, 193; and public servants/service, 124, 152; and Québec, 192, 193; and the West, 193
Truman, Harry, 197
"trust[ing] the people," 205, 206, 207
Les Trusts Général, 27
Tupper, Sir Charles, 39, 40, 41, 43
Tupper, Sir Charles Hibbert, 43
Turner, John Napier, 6, 31, 158
24 Sussex Drive, 174
two-nations doctrine, 190, 195

Unemployment Insurance Act, 177
unilingualism, 188
unionists, 45
Union Nationale (UN), 14, 15–19, 191–192
unions, 52, 53, 63, 78, 114, 117, 143; in Britain, 68, 69; in France, 70, 71
United Farmers of Canada, 50

United Kingdom. *See* Britain
United Nations, 95
universality of social programs, 124
universal suffrage, 113, 117–119
universities, 181
U.S.: budget secrecy in, 126; committees in, 155; and Iran hostage question, 180–181; leadership selection in, 3, 37, 44–45, 47, 49, 53, 54–66, 72, 110–111, 114; policy agendas in, 202; presidential cabinet in, 201; public servants/service in, 153, 170–171, 176; savings and loan crisis, 206; and taxation without representation, 124, 125–126
U.S. constitution, 194

Verchères (Que.) riding, 108
volunteer labour, vs. contributions, 115
votes of confidence/non-confidence, 101, 103–104, 138–140

Wagner, Claude, 27, 92, 93, 192–193; 1976 leadership bid, 79, 80, 82–83, 85, 86, 87
western Canada, 47, 124, 194, 197
Western Progressive Movement, 90
white papers, 145
White, Sir Thomas, 43, 44
Willison, J. J., 44–45
Wilson, Michael, 124, 141, 147
Winters, Robert, 138
women, 57, 84, 85
Woodsworth, J. S., 50, 51
working-class representation, 84; *See also* blue-collar workers; unions
Worthington, Peter, 28
Wray, Joseph, 95